D1385640

Troubled Waters

THE CHANGING FORTUNES OF
WHALES AND DOLPHINS

Sarah Lazarus

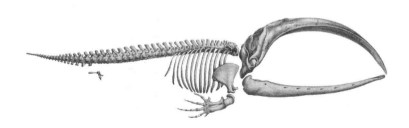

Published by the Natural History Museum, London

For Neale

First published by the Natural History Museum, Cromwell Road, London
SW7 5BD

© Natural History Museum, London, 2006

ISBN: 0 565 09192 1
ISBN 13: 978 09192 7

A catalogue record for this book is available from the British Library.

Edited by Celia Coyne
Index by Angie Hipkin
Designed by Mercer Design
Typeset by Fakenham Photosetting
Reproduction and printing by St Edmundsbury Press

Distribution

NBN International
Estover Road
Devon PL6 7PY
UK

Contents

Acknowledgements

I would like to thank the many experts who kindly commented on sections of the manuscript, provided information and answered my endless questions: Christian Antonioli, Michael Barkham, Biju Basil, Isabel Beasley, John Bockstoce, Ezra Clark, Tetsuya Endo, Jim Estes, Cindy Gibbons, Peter Gill, Jonathan Gordon, Frances Gulland, Michael Jasny, Robert Kenney, Darlene Ketten, Kristen Koyama, Daniel Martineau, Brenna McLeod, Michael Noad, Simon Northridge, Adam Pack, Steve Palumbi, Clare Perry, August Pfluger, Rebecca Regnery, Dale Rice, Ali Ross, Peter Ross, Vicky Rowntree, Dave Rugh, Robert Suydam, Steven Swartz, Hans Thewissen, Heather Trim, Hal Whitehead, Cathy Williamson, Bernd Würsig and Sharon Young. Any errors that remain are, of course, entirely my own responsibility.

I am especially grateful to Mark Simmonds, Director of Science for the Whale and Dolphin Conservation Society; Naomi Rose, Marine Mammal Scientist for the Humane Society of the

United States; and Erich Hoyt, Co-director of the Far East Russia Orca Project and Senior Research Fellow with the Whale and Dolphin Conservation Society, who reviewed large sections of the manuscript and were incredibly generous with their time, wisdom and energy.

A big thank you to the team at the Natural History Museum and particularly to Trudy Brannan who oversaw the writing of the book from beginning to end. I am immensely grateful for her guidance and insight. Thanks also to Celia Coyne for doing such a brilliant job with the editing.

Heartfelt thanks to all the friends who have lent support and assistance at different stages in the writing process: Sarah Adams, Louise Cowley, James Kerr, Keren Levy, Victoria Millar, Holly Pelham, Emma Ross and John Waller. Extra special thanks go to Samanthi Dissanayake who read and commented on most of the chapters and provided invaluable input throughout.

My beautiful baby Poppy made no small contribution by delaying her own arrival in this world until I had first delivered the manuscript. Biggest thanks of all go to my husband Neale for his constant encouragement, support and inspiration, and for reading every word I wrote. This book is dedicated to him with all my love.

Introduction

A whale of a tale

O N A BRIGHT, WINTRY DAY in January 2006, a northern bottlenose whale lost its way and swam up the River Thames into central London. It meandered slowly upstream, cruising past the iconic landmarks that line the river: the Tower of London, St Paul's Cathedral and Big Ben. Londoners were thrilled to see such an imposing and unfamiliar wild animal at close quarters in the centre of their city and excited onlookers crowded along the river's banks. But their jubilation soon turned to dismay. The animal was seen to be bleeding profusely from a head wound and on a couple of occasions it ran aground.

A rescue team hastened to the scene and hauled the exhausted whale onto an inflatable raft. They were carrying the whale back downriver to the open sea when it convulsed and died. A few days later an autopsy revealed that the whale, a female, had suffered a combination of dehydration, kidney failure and muscle damage. During her days in the river she had been unable to feed on the deep-water squid that usually provided her with water. It was suggested that having wandered off course, the whale had been lured up the Thames by the pull of her homing instincts guiding her west towards her native waters of the North Atlantic.

Before the autopsy results were published various explanations for the whale's unexpected appearance and unhappy demise were proposed. Perhaps an infestation of parasites or the consumption of highly contaminated food had weakened the whale's immune system and she had fallen victim to a crippling disease. Or perhaps, being extremely sensitive to sound, she had been deafened by naval sonar testing or disoriented by noisy boat traffic. Maybe she been injured by deep-sea commercial fishing gear while foraging for squid; or perhaps climate change was to blame, affecting the Gulf Stream and other ocean currents so that distribution of the whale's prey had altered and led her away from traditional hunting grounds. These speculations were dismissed as soon as the facts became known, but in the interim the plethora of possible causes came as a surprise to many people who were unaware that such tragedies are increasingly commonplace.

Whales and their close relatives dolphins and porpoises, collectively known as cetaceans, swim in troubled waters. Their changing fortunes are inextricably linked to our own history. Human activity, shaped by wider technological, cultural and political forces, exerts a considerable influence on these wonderful animals. For centuries whales and dolphins were regarded as nothing more than an economic resource. When a whale swam up the Thames in 1658, gleeful locals hurried to the river's shores – but on this occasion they simply hacked the animal to death.

Our current relationship with whales and dolphins is both paradoxical and puzzling. Interest in them is at an all time high. It is hard to define their special appeal, but it could stem from the fact that they are delightfully familiar and yet totally alien. We identify with their intelligence, sociality and sentience, but they inhabit a cold, dark and largely unknown realm more hostile to human life than outer space. The last few decades have seen an explosion in the number of research and conservation projects dedicated to studying and saving whales and dolphins. Opportunities to swim with dolphins or go whale-watching draw thousands of visitors, books of beautiful photography adorn countless coffee tables, their songs are recorded and sold on CDs and their images appear on everything from jewellery to the marketing for beer, airlines and life insurance. Our enthusiasm for these captivating creatures was perfectly illustrated by the public's compassionate response to London's lost whale.

Yet there is a contradiction in our relationship with whales and dolphins. For all the positive feelings that these wild animals inspire, our actions continue to affect them negatively. As the conjecture surrounding the London whale revealed, human activities now intrude on their lives in all sorts of ways. Many people feel a deep appreciation for cetaceans, but remain largely unaware of their predicament.

Historically our impact on whales and dolphins was direct and intentional. Prosecuted without limitation or dispute, whaling in centuries past brought several species to the brink of extinction. Those animals lucky enough to evade the hunter's harpoon continued their lives free of human interference. Today the dynamic looks very different. The ways in which we affect cetaceans are complex and multi-dimensional. Often there is no intention to harm them, but they are threatened as an unfortunate consequence of the way we live.

Whales and dolphins are still deliberately killed. Commercial whaling is a politically charged and highly controversial issue that receives widespread media coverage. But hunting is not the greatest threat they face. Hundreds of thousands of animals perish in commercial fishing nets every year or are struck by ships. As global warming melts the polar ice-caps, as the seas absorb poisonous man-made chemicals, as the oceans resound with man-made noise and marine habitats are degraded, whales and dolphins face myriad and mounting pressures.

The World Conservation Union (IUCN) produces the definitive *Red List of Threatened Species*. Two cetaceans are currently registered as 'critically endangered' – a category reserved for species that face an extremely high risk of extinction in the near future. One is the baiji or Chinese river dolphin, an enigmatic inhabitant of China's Yangtze river. The other is the vaquita, a petite porpoise that lives in Mexico's Gulf of California. Several species appear in the next category, 'endangered'. Their risk of extinction, although great, is less immediate. Of this group the North Atlantic right whale causes the most concern. Just 300 of these slow-swimming behemoths roam the waters off the east coast of North America. Although completely protected from hunting, they now fall victim to the twin perils of fishing nets and ship strikes and their prospects are far from rosy.

But it's not all doom and gloom. There is much greater awareness of the plight of whales and dolphins than ever before. Initiatives to conserve them are flourishing. Several species that once looked consigned to the history books by unregulated whaling are on the road to recovery. More than 26,000 gray whales parade down North America's west coast every year on their annual migration. The blue whale of the northern hemisphere, the southern right whale and many populations of the whale watcher's favourite, the humpback whale, also appear to be making a comeback.

Whales and dolphins are important not simply because they are popular and interesting animals. They are situated at the top of the food chain, so their well-being signals the health of the whole marine environment. Their future will be determined not by our sentiments but by our actions. The problems they face are diverse and escalating and it is time to consider the ways in which we exploit, pollute or protect their ocean home.

In the beginning

On the evolution of whales and dolphins

WHALES, DOLPHINS AND PORPOISES are collectively known as cetaceans. Their name derives from *ketos* – Greek for sea monster – although cetaceans are in fact mammals. They are special, because of all the mammals on Earth, cetaceans are the best adapted for life in water. A whale gliding past an iceberg, or a dolphin bow-riding in front of a boat, seems as comfortable in its element as any fish. Some species traverse the oceans on epic migrations, some have spectacular diving abilities and can plunge to abyssal depths in minutes, while others navigate and hunt in rivers that are so murky their eyesight has become redundant. None can live on dry land. Yet like all mammals they breathe air, the blood in their veins is warm and they give birth to live young, which they nurse with mother's milk.

The groups of animals that we call 'whales', 'dolphins' and 'porpoises' are not as clearly defined as their names imply. Generally speaking whales are huge, dolphins are medium-sized and porpoises are small, but there are exceptions in all cases. Some large dolphins are bigger than small whales and some whales, such as the pilot whale, are in fact dolphins. To add to the confusion, in the USA all small cetaceans are commonly referred to as porpoises.

Their scientific classification is much more straightforward. All cetaceans fit tidily into two groups: odontocetes, or toothed whales, which have teeth; and mysticetes, or baleen whales, which do not. Mysticetes include some of the largest animals on the planet such as the blue whale, humpback whale and right whale. With the notable exception of the sperm whale, they tend to be bigger than odontocetes, which include the narwhal, beluga whale, beaked whales, oceanic dolphins, river dolphins and all the porpoises. The mysticetes and the sperm whale are informally referred to as the great whales.

There are about 85 species of cetacean although no one is sure exactly how many – the opinions of experts sometimes differ, and new information can overturn what was previously established as fact. As a group, cetaceans are incredibly diverse. They live in rivers and oceans, from the equator to the poles, in water that ranges in temperature from 30°C to −2°C (86°F to 28.4°F). Some dwell in flooded tropical forests and some hunt in deep-sea canyons; some hug coastlines and others live in such distant waters that they do not spy land once in their entire lives. They range in size from the tiny vaquita, a 1.2 m (4 ft) long porpoise, to the blue whale, a true colossus at over 30 m (100 ft). Many are brown or grey, some have splashes of colour, spots and stripes, and a few are a monochrome vision in black and white.

Studying cetaceans is inherently difficult. They often live far out to sea, travel long distances and spend much of their lives beneath the water's surface. Fifty years ago our knowledge of their biology and behaviour comprised a jumble of anecdotes, whalers' observations and the occasional study conducted on a beach-cast specimen. Since then research has expanded dramatically. Captive animals provide opportunities for close-up examination and studies in the wild are growing ever more sophisticated. A range of exciting new technologies has supplemented the tried and tested technique of collecting information using binoculars and a notebook. Researchers attach satellite tags to animals and track their movements, observe their hidden lives via deep-water video probes, obtain skin and blubber samples using biopsy darts and listen to the sounds they make with directional hydrophones. The ability to analyse DNA and decode genes is of tremendous significance and has contributed to an overhaul of cetacean taxonomy. In 2002 DNA tests revealed the true identity of a species that was entirely new to science: Perrin's beaked whale. Beaked whales are an especially elusive group; many spend their lives in remote waters and have never been seen alive. Known only

Researchers place a satellite tag on a gray whale in Baja California, Mexico.

from remains washed up on far-flung beaches, they are thought to be the most poorly understood of all large mammalian species. Such was the case with Perrin's beaked whale. Between 1975 and 1997 five cetaceans were found dead on the coast of southern California. Based on anatomical studies, the first four arrivals were wrongly identified as Hector's beaked whales and the fifth as a baby Cuvier's beaked whale. Almost 30 years after the first animal was examined, genetic analysis revealed that all five animals were actually members of the same species although their DNA did not match that of any known whale. A new cetacean had been discovered and it was called Perrin's beaked whale.

The fact that the existence of Perrin's beaked whale came to light so recently underlines the huge gaps in our knowledge. Despite a substantial swell in the flow of information about cetaceans and a widespread fascination for them, the details of their lives in the deep blue remain a mystery. The more that is discovered the more we realise there is yet to understand about these extraordinary animals.

WHALES AND DOLPHINS are such superbly evolved aquatic creatures it is hard to imagine that their forebears walked on land. To understand how they came into being it is necessary to turn the clock back 50 million years. For decades fossil evidence was thin on the ground and scientists could only speculate as to their origins. In the absence of clear intermediate forms numerous prehistoric mammals were proposed as ancestors. Then in the 1980s and 1990s a remarkable series of fossil finds lifted the veil on the whales' distant past.

The early cetaceans are collectively known as archaeocetes, which means the first whales. Although there is still some debate, the latest thinking is that the archaeocetes descended from a group of hoofed mammals called the artiodactyls. Fossil evidence, backed up by DNA studies, indicate that the present-day artiodactyls – hippos, pigs, camels, deer, sheep, goats and cattle – are the closest living relatives of modern whales and dolphins.

The earliest known archaeocete, *Pakicetus*, did not look like a whale and did not live in the sea. Its fossilised remains have been recovered from ancient rock beds in the foothills of the Himalayas. This area, which extends into India and Pakistan, is considered the cradle of whale evolution. Although no single complete skeleton has yet been found, palaeontologists have surmised from dozens of specimens that *Pakicetus* was a heavy-set animal somewhere between the size of a fox and a wolf. It bore no visible resemblance to its marine descendants but an unusual piece of bone in the ear region, found in cetaceans and no other animals, clearly indicates its relationship to them.

Fifty million years ago, during the time of *Pakicetus*, the landscape looked very different from today. A long, shallow arm of water called the Tethys Seaway extended from what is now central

Despite walking on four legs, *Pakicetus* is the earliest known whale.

Asia to southern Europe. Towards the interior of the landmass shallow rivers and ephemeral streams scored the terrain. *Pakicetus* probably waded into these freshwater rivers to hunt for food and returned to their banks to rest. It shared its home with early marsupials, bats, rodents, hoofed animals and our own ancestors — squirrel-sized primates.

About a million years later *Ambulocetus natans* took up life at the edge of sea. The 'walking swimming whale' was similar in size to a large male sea lion. It was a powerful animal with a cumbersome head, broad chest, strong muscular back, big tail and squat legs. Its four-toed feet were long and paddle-shaped, and its hands had five fingers, each tipped with a little hoof. This beast could amble, albeit clumsily, on land but was probably more at home in the water. It swam like a modern otter, thrusting its hind limbs through the water and undulating its spine and tail for extra propulsion. Lurking in brackish swamps and briny estuaries the walking swimming whale hunted like a modern crocodile — pouncing on unsuspecting prey and dispatching them with a snap of its mighty jaws.

After this the archaeocetes diversified. They expanded from their homeland and fanned out through the tropics. The benefits of aquatic life must have been considerable because the transition to a fully marine existence occurred in just 10 million years — the blink of an eye on the evolutionary timescale. During this period they crossed a critical metabolic threshold. Most land mammals cannot survive without access to fresh water but cetaceans can. Instead of drinking water they obtain it from their prey as well as retaining water produced by metabolic processes that would otherwise be exhaled on the breath. However, to avoid dehydration they also need to process and expel large quantities of salt. Exactly how they do that remains something of a mystery but it is assumed that their kidneys became specially adapted for this purpose.

Basilosaurus was the first truly marine cetacean.

The earliest archaeocetes to spend their whole lives in water without setting foot on land were the basilosaurids. The first such fossil recovered was examined by Richard Harlan, an American physician, in 1843. The ancient animal he observed more closely resembled a mythical sea serpent than a modern whale. Forgivably Harlan assumed it to be a giant reptile and named it *Basilosaurus*, meaning 'king lizard'. The misnomer persists because according to the rules of taxonomy once a name has been appointed it cannot be easily changed. The basilosaurids were a diverse group. Some, like Dr Harlan's specimen, had elongated snake-like bodies up to 20 m (66 ft) in length. Others were much shorter and more compact.

In order to take to the sea the early whales had to adapt. Their bodies became more tapered and streamlined so that water flowed smoothly along their contours and they could swim with agility and grace. By now whales had developed the tough tapering wings at the end of their tails – known as flukes – which provide thrust when they swim. The hindlimbs had dwindled to small vestiges because the basilosaurids did not need to support their own bodies. These evolutionary remnants, souvenirs inherited from their land-bound ancestors, may have been used as claspers when the animals mated. In modern whales the hindlimbs are tiny splint-like bones kept encased under the skin but the ancient genetic code is still present and very rarely a freak whale is born that has sprouted one or two external legs.

The basilosaurids were the first cetaceans able to reproduce entirely at sea. Modern cetaceans give birth underwater after between ten and 17 months of pregnancy. The female then nudges her calf to the surface for its momentous first breath. To start with she lies on her side near the surface of the water as the calf suckles so that it can breathe air at the same time. Later, when it has mastered the art holding its breath, it feeds under-water. The intimate bond between mother and baby lasts for life in some species and in others is severed within a year.

As time passed the archaeocetes became ever more suited to their marine existence. Arms reduced and modified into flippers that balanced their bodies in the water. The nostrils migrated upwards. Basilosaurids had to poke the tips of their noses out of the water to breathe but in modern cetaceans the nostrils have become blowholes on the tops of their heads so they can inhale and exhale without having to lift their heads. Odontocetes have a single blowhole while mysticetes have two. The shape, angle and height of the 'blows' produced when the animal exhales differ in each species and allow experienced whalers, scientists and whale-watchers to identify them from a distance. The archaeocetes also piled on fat in the form of blubber – a generous layer under the skin that insulates and acts as an energy store. Blubber ensures that whales and dolphins stay warm even in frigid waters. In fact blubber is so efficient that cetaceans can easily overheat. In order to avoid this, the animal's circulation can alter so that blood is pumped through the body's extremities, particularly the flippers and flukes, bypassing the blubber and taking advantage of the chilling effects of water.

Another crucial skill that the cetaceans developed is the ability to dive. Their talent in this regard is awesome. The human world free-diving record, attained with the help of a weighted sled and buoyancy control device, is 172 m (564 ft). Most cetaceans can reach such depths unaided in the first few months of life. The northern bottlenose whale regularly descends 1.5 km (almost 1 mile) for over an hour. Sperm whales currently hold the cetacean world record of 2 km (1¼ miles).

Diving whales and dolphins need to be able to hold their breath for long periods of time, store sufficient oxygen to function and resist immense hydrostatic pressures. They overcome these daunting challenges in a number of ways. As the animal dives its heart rate and metabolism slow and blood is shunted to the vital organs, conserving precious oxygen. Cetaceans can store far larger amounts of oxygen than land mammals because their blood is rich in haemoglobin and their muscles contain elevated levels of myoglobin. These proteins bind to oxygen and release it slowly during the long dives. The whales' lungs withstand pressure by gradually folding up and collapsing as the animal descends.

For the first whales the challenges of marine life were great but the advantages were greater still. The sea teemed with prey and offered endless space. Nourished by plentiful food and buoyed by water the new cetaceans diversified and prospered.

AROUND 35 MILLION YEARS AGO the mysticetes and odontocetes began to split from each other. The mysticetes developed filter feeding and the odontocetes acquired echolocation. These two very different feeding strategies made both groups the exceptionally successful marine predators that we see today.

The mysticetes lost their teeth and instead grew baleen plates – long rigid structures draped with hairy fronds that hang from the upper jaw. With this modification came an entirely new style of feeding. Baleen whales engulf large volumes of water and prey and expel the water through the plates. These act as a giant filter, trapping the food. Filter feeding allows the whales to ingest massive quantities and fuels their unrivalled growth.

Right whales and bowhead whales are 'skimmers' – they cruise through clouds of animal plankton near the surface and skim off prey from the stream of water that pours over the baleen. Blue, fin and minke whales are 'gulpers'. They drop their lower jaws and lunge into dense shoals of crustaceans or small fish such as herring and sardines.

Other mysticetes have developed their own harvesting systems. Gray whales sieve mud from the ocean floor for crustaceans while humpback whales often gather to feed in groups. Up to 22 animals have been observed launching a collective attack on a huge ball of fish. The whales amass beneath the fish then make a synchronised charge for the surface, probably in response to a vocal signal by one of the group. Unable to flee in any direction the fish are easily devoured. Humpbacks also trap fish schools by encircling them and releasing a steady chain of bubbles from their blowholes – the bubbles form nets of air through which the prey cannot escape.

While mysticetes produced the ultimate natural sieving system, odontocetes developed echolocation – a biological form of sonar. Toothed whales and dolphins emit an intense beam of high-frequency sound that bounces off an object and returns as an echo. By interpreting the echo the animal can determine the object's distance and size. In this way odontocetes perceive their environment with three-dimensional clarity. Freed from dependence on eyesight they can chase and catch prey in total darkness. This ability allows them to navigate and exploit a vast range of habitats including the dark oceanic depths where sunlight never penetrates, and the opaquely silted waters of rivers and coastlines. The majority of species eat fish, squid and crustaceans. They pursue individual prey and swallow them whole. Unlike most terrestrial mammals and their own ancestors, which have assorted teeth with different functions, most odontocetes have uniform cone-shaped pegs. There is enormous disparity in the number of teeth, and size and shape can vary too. The spinner dolphin has the most, its long jaw carrying between 180 and 256 teeth. Species with plenty of teeth tend to seize slippery prey and gulp them down without chewing. At the other end of the scale a number of species, mostly belonging to the beaked whale family, have only two teeth. In females these may remain permanently embedded in the jawbone so for all practical purposes they have no teeth at all. Species like these usually use their tongues to suction prey into their mouths.

There are a few striking anomalies. The male narwhal has a single long tooth that looks like a unicorn's horn. In females neither of the two teeth erupt but in males the left tooth pierces the upper lip and grows spiralling anticlockwise into a 3 m (10 ft) long tusk. The males sometimes use the tooth to fence with rivals, each trying to out-spar his opponent with his unwieldy dental appendage. Male strap-toothed whales have a similarly curious arrangement. Two teeth emerge from the middle of the lower jaw and curl upwards and inwards extending over the top of the upper jaw. In older animals the teeth sometimes meet in the middle forming a muzzle and preventing the animal from opening its jaw more than a few centimetres. Fortunately the strap-toothed whale is a suction feeder and this impediment does not prevent it from catching its favoured prey, squid.

The different feeding strategies of mysticetes and odontocetes influence the formation of their societies. Baleen whales tend to mingle casually on their feeding grounds since their prey is fairly evenly distributed. Among the toothed cetaceans there is greater variety; some species are rather solitary but many congregate in vast numbers to exploit dense patches of food. Fish and crustaceans are not evenly spread throughout the oceans; instead they mass around 'upwellings' where streams of nutrient-rich water surge from the ocean floor. Larger predators follow in their wake. Assemblies of mixed species of oceanic dolphins, often numbering in their thousands, are not uncommon.

The threat of predation is another influence in cetacean society. Many baleen whales dedicate the summer months to feeding in polar waters but come the winter they migrate to distant temperate or tropical regions. Here they fraternise, court, mate and bear their calves. Some migrations are true odysseys. For many years the gray whale, which can clock up 20,000 km (12,000 miles) on its annual round trip from Alaska to Baja California, Mexico, was thought to undertake the longest migration of any mammal but researchers tracing the voyages of humpback whales have recently discovered that they may travel even greater distances. There has been extensive speculation about the reasons for these lengthy expeditions. Food is often scarce at the breeding grounds and the roving whales spend a large proportion of their energy reserves making the journey so there should be compelling advantages. Conventional explanations suggest that newborn calves are better able to survive in warm, calm waters; or that the routes followed represent unbroken traditions developed during previous eras when the continents were closer together. However, in recent years the conundrum has been re-examined and it is now thought that the risk of predation may play a significant role.

Until the first harpoon struck its deadly blow the only predator most cetaceans routinely encountered was one of their own – the orca. Also known as the killer whale, the orca lives in tightly knit, stable groups based on maternal kinship. The groups, or pods, make highly coordinated attacks on larger species in much the same way as a pride of lions or pack of wild dogs cooperates to hunt big game on the plains of Africa.

Attacks on blue, sei and gray whales have been reported and the bodies and tail flukes of humpback whales are often raked with orca tooth marks. The frequency and success rates of these assaults are unknown but the sheer size of adult mysticetes affords them protection, while their thrashing tail flukes are formidable enough to repel the most persistent of adversaries. Young whales are extremely vulnerable, however, and it is for their protection that adults may travel such long distances to lower latitudes where reduced numbers of orcas mean that their newborns will be relatively safe.

Odontocetes are more nomadic than migratory. Their large social groups may provide safety in numbers but if an individual is attacked by orcas, or in some cases sharks, they have only their speed in the water to rely on. One species, the sperm whale, adopts more tactical defence strategies. Occasionally they blind their assailants by releasing clouds of faeces. This behaviour curiously parallels that of squid, their principal prey, which often attempt to escape under cover of gushing black ink. The sperm whale's primary ploy, however, involves cooperation and mutual support. Females live together in groups of about ten with attendant calves. The mothers are forced to leave their vulnerable offspring at the surface while they feed at great depths because the young animals are not capable of making such ambitious descents. The mothers ensure that there is always an adult present to babysit by diving at different times. If predators approach, the whales often react by forming a defensive circle, their tail flukes facing outwards with young or wounded animals shielded in the centre. Although this behaviour is effective at repelling orcas, it was a boon to whalers, who were delighted to find their quarries clustered on the spot and did not scatter to save themselves.

BY AROUND FOUR MILLION YEARS AGO the whales and dolphins we see today were starting to emerge. Continually refining their adaptations they colonised all the world's oceans and seas and some of its rivers, becoming ever more specialised for a waterborne life. Unsurpassed by any other mammal in this regard they invaded and conquered the blue planet.

Blubber, baleen and liquid gold

On the early history of whaling

FOR MUCH OF HISTORY hunting whales was a dirty and dangerous business. To set sail in a small boat and slaughter a huge and probably furious leviathan with minimal technology is no mean feat. But as a natural resource, whales have no equal. The risks may be great, but the rewards are greater still.

Whales are a hunter's dream. Built on a different scale to terrestrial quarry, these marine mammals yield a massive quantity of spoils. And unlike domestic livestock and crops they do not need nurturing and cultivating – they can simply be harvested. When whaling first became an industry the world's seas were brimming with them. To the hunters the whales seemed like fat floating treasure chests, idly waiting to be plucked from the water and plundered for their precious bounty. By landing a single great whale they reaped a vast mound of meat, barrel-loads of indispensable oil and racks of valuable baleen.

The history of commercial whaling has been shaped by economics, technology and the biology and behaviour of the whales themselves. Early on the industry developed in a piecemeal fashion – springing up in far-flung parts of the world, at times dominated by different nations and focusing on different whale species. But despite their many variations, most whaling enterprises followed a well-documented and very simple pattern. Each one began with the discovery of new whale stocks. Hunters flocked to the scene, all hoping to seize the most whales. Success came easily, profits poured in and the industry flourished. But the whales were overexploited. Whale stocks tend to crash rapidly because, like all cetaceans, whales are especially vulnerable on account of their biology – they take years to mature, reproduce extremely slowly and invest heavily in each calf. As a result they cannot easily replenish losses. When profits started dropping the whalers moved on. They sought fruitful new pastures, relentlessly decimating one whale population after another. Inevitably bust followed boom – all the whales were gone or there were insufficient numbers left to make their pursuit worthwhile.

In this way many of the world's whale stocks were driven to the very brink of extinction. Falling returns and lost investments aroused consternation, but it is only recently that whales have received adequate protection from commercial hunting. Some species have made promising recoveries while others remain in a critical state and face an uncertain future.

EVER SINCE PEOPLE STARTED living by the sea they have encountered the occasional whale stranded on the shore. A dead whale was a windfall: it yielded generous stockpiles of nutritious meat and fat; sinews for sewing clothes and fishing lines; and bones for making houses, furniture, tools, weapons and boats. The Icelandic word *hvalreki*, now used to cheer a lottery win, translates to 'beached whale' – a reminder of the days when the jackpot was a cetacean carcass.

Eventually certain maritime communities started actively pursuing whales rather than waiting for them to drift ashore. Images etched into rock faces in Norway and Korea testify that cetaceans were hunted as long ago as 6000 BC. The Norwegians, in particular, were whaling pioneers. They shepherded schools of whales along narrow, sheer-walled fjords towards shallow beaches where they could be easily dispatched with long knives and lances. A nation of sea raiders, their techniques travelled with them to colonies in the Hebrides, Orkney, Shetland and Faroe Islands. In the Faroes hundreds of pilot whales are still killed in a similar way every year.

Makah Indians whaling in the traditional style off the west coast of North America in 1883.

Different methods predominated in other parts of the world. Hunters from various cultures living around the northwest Pacific focused their efforts on the art of poisoning. Attacking whales from small boats in the open sea, they speared them with lances daubed with aconite, a highly toxic plant extract. Though deadly this strategy didn't always prove successful. The hunters had to rely on winds and currents to wash the carcass ashore once the poison had taken effect, which meant that many kills were lost at sea.

Another ancient technology left less to chance and would become the future weapon of choice: the harpoon. Harpoon-wielding Inuit and Native Americans pursued bowhead whales, grays and humpbacks in canoes. The harpoon, thrust into a whale's back, was attached to a brightly painted wooden drum or sealskin. The colourful bouncing float slowed the whale's progress and revealed its course to the hunters. As the whale tired the hunters drew gradually closer until the stricken beast was in reach of their spears.

What all these practices had in common was that they operated at the subsistence level, supplying small groups with the food, clothing and shelter they needed to survive. The impact on whale populations was minimal. It was only with the advent of commercial whaling – when whale products became tradable commodities that could be sold for profit – that the widespread slaughter really began.

COMMERCIAL WHALING STARTED with just one group of people, the Basques, and just one whale, the North Atlantic right whale.

The Basques began their assault on the right whale in the Bay of Biscay off the coasts of Spain and France around the tenth century. They adopted the same harpoon technique that had been used in Arctic regions for centuries, scanning the sea for whales from lookouts and launching small flotillas of boats to intercept them. They stabbed their prey with harpoons and finished them off with lances.

Whalers gave the right whale its common name, describing it as the 'right' whale to hunt. From a whaler's point of view there was much that was right about the right whale. Its bulky, rotund black body, mottled by distinctive callosities – pale patches created by crowds of tiny whale lice – made it easy to identify. A slow swimmer that passes by close to the shore, the whale was relatively easy to chase in a boat and, obligingly, it floats when dead.

At first Basque whaling was a local concern. The right whale yielded a dizzying variety of useful products: meat for consumption, oil for lighting, giant vertebrae that were fashioned into chairs, ribs that were transformed into fence pickets and house beams, and excrement that gave forth a red dye. As time went on demand for the most valuable whale products – oil, meat and later baleen – grew so the Basques started trading them. In the absence of refrigeration the meat was preserved with salt and stored and transported in barrels. Whaling transformed from a subsistence activity, limited by the community's needs, to a commercial enterprise dictated by market forces. Now that there was money to be made the only potential constraints were consumer demand and the number of whales in the sea.

Whale oil is extracted from blubber. Right whales, like all cetaceans, are cocooned by this thick layer of fat. Blubber consists of a honeycomb of large balloon-like cells filled with oil. The cells are held in place by a collagen mesh that makes the blubber firm and tough, rather than flabby. The blubber streamlines the whale's body, providing smooth contours so it can glide through the water with minimal resistance. Blubber floats in water, so its thickness is limited to ensure that the whale is not too buoyant to dive. The right whale has extremely thick blubber, which accounts for both its leisurely swimming pace and its popularity as a marketable resource.

Blubber acts as a fatty envelope of insulation. Cetaceans are warm-blooded and like land mammals need to maintain a stable core body temperature of around 37°C (99°F). However, their environment is often extremely cold. In polar seas temperatures can be as low as −2°C (28°F), and water conducts heat away from a warm body 25 times faster than air. The blubber keeps the animal warm, cushioning its inner organs against the bone-chilling cold of the ocean. Blubber also acts as a supply of reserve energy for migratory species like the right whale. The oil can be broken down to provide vital sustenance as the whale travels long distances from its feeding grounds to breeding, calving and wintering sites where food is scarce.

Before mineral oil and natural gas were discovered the oil stored in whale blubber was a vital and versatile commodity. It illuminated the streets and domestic residences of cities all over Europe and later North America, and was also used in the manufacture of wool and leather. But the right whale surrendered another material that became even more valuable than the oil: whalebone. Whalebone is the name misleadingly given to baleen – the plates that hang from the roof of the mouth of mysticete whales. The plates, held in place by dense rubbery gum tissue, are arranged in a row down each side of the mouth. Some species have more plates than others. Right whales are close to the top of the scale with between 400 and 600 plates, each one about 2.5 m (8 ft) long. The baleen plates grow continuously throughout the whale's life, sprouting out from the base and wearing away at the edges. As the outer layers become worn the long fibrous tubules inside are exposed and hang down, forming a hairy fringe. When the whale expels water from its mouth through the gaps between the plates, these curtains filter and trap the food.

Rather than bone baleen is made of keratin – the same substance found in fingernails, hair, hooves, horns and claws. It became indispensable because of two important properties: it is tough yet flexible, and when immersed in hot water it becomes pliant and can be moulded. These qualities made it an excellent material for manufacturing a vast assortment of goods including fishing rods, whip handles, sweeps' brushes, chair seats, shoehorns and umbrella spokes. Whalebone also became a fashion essential used to make corsets, bustles, bodices, collars, ruffs and hoop skirts, and to stiffen the curls in elaborate wigs.

Markets for right whale products were established across Europe throughout the 12th and 13th centuries. As profits soared more and more Basque merchants entered the business. But as the enterprise expanded, so the right whales declined. Although each port captured only a small number of whales each year, fewer and fewer whales were spotted cruising alongside the Biscayan coast. A solution presented itself in the early years of the 16th century when Basque fishermen catching cod near the island of Newfoundland reported finding seas positively teeming with whales.

The whalers set sail, stationed themselves on Canada's Labrador Coast and continued whaling with renewed vigour. They captured the right whale and its close relative, the bowhead, as they migrated through the Strait of Belle Isle, the turbulent stretch of water between the mainland and Newfoundland. By this time the Basques had adopted a new method of hunting to prevent harpooned whales simply speeding off over the horizon, as they often did. They attached the whaleboat to the harpoon with a long line and used the boat as a restraining float. The line paid out as the whale fled and could be gradually hauled in as the animal tired. This technique was far more dangerous but considerably more efficient.

Once killed, the whales were towed to shore for processing. The blubber was stripped, or flensed, from the carcass and chopped into small pieces. The oil was then extracted by melting the blubber in large copper cauldrons perched on tryworks – a series of stone fire boxes lining the beach. Next the liquid oil was ladled into storage barrels in which the pure oil floated to the top while the impurities, known as 'dross', settled on the bottom. Eventually the rendered and purified oil was transferred to oak and beech casks ready for shipping.

Archaeologists have unearthed a hoard of relics that paint a picture of a whaleman's life in this rugged, remote outpost. The coopers who assembled the storage casks usually lived and worked in rudimentary buildings located near the tryworks. Most crew members lived on their ships, which remained anchored in the harbour throughout the season. Excavations have retrieved the tools of their trade as well as personal possessions such as drinking glasses, ceramics and wooden rosary beads. A whaler's life was far from easy. Along with the intense cold and discomfort there was the constant threat of death by drowning. Testament to this is a windswept whaler's cemetery discovered in 1982 on a small hump of wave-drenched rock called Saddle Island. It is the final resting place of more than 140 Basque whalemen who never made it home.

By the end of the 16th century history was already starting to repeat itself. The annual procession of whales through the Strait of Belle Isle had dwindled to a trickle. Around the same time the maritime economy of the Spanish Basques suffered a recession as a consequence of lengthy wars that were taking place in Europe. Basque whaling supremacy was coming to an end, but elsewhere the slaughter was only just beginning.

IN 1596 A FORTUNE-SEEKING Dutch navigator called Willem Barents embarked on a voyage to find the fabled Northeast Passage that would allow ships to travel from the Atlantic to the Pacific via the Arctic Ocean. Although he failed in his mission he did succeed in discovering Spitsbergen, a barren, mountainous, glacier-shrouded archipelago 1000 km (600 miles) south of the North Pole. He reported home that the icy seas surrounding Spitsbergen thronged with bowhead whales.

The bowhead was an even greater prize than its southern cousin the right whale. Longer and considerably stouter, it has the thickest blubber of any whale – up to 70 cm (28 in) in places – to insulate it against the bitingly cold Arctic waters. It is also generously endowed with that most valuable of commodities: baleen. The bowhead's capacious bow-shaped mouth, from which it derives its name, contains up to 720 plates of baleen, each measuring over 4 m (13 ft) in length.

Fifteen years after Barents first encountered the Spitsbergen bowheads the British outfitted a fleet and set out to bring the bounty home. Jonas Poole, the fleet's captain, was amazed at the plenitude of whales:

"The whales lay so thicke about the ship that some ran against our cables, some against the ship, and one against the rudder. One lay under our beake-head and slept there for a long while."

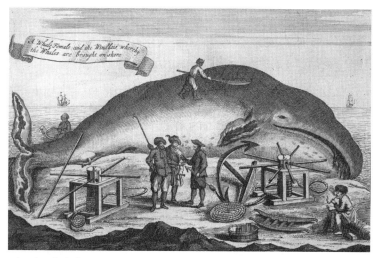

A bowhead whale winched ashore in Spitsbergen, 1744.

A year later the Dutch caught up with them. Both nations were determined to gain control over the Greenland fishery, as it was then known, and interspersed their whaling with warfare. Things came to a head around 1618 when the British fleet, having concentrated all its efforts on trouncing the Dutch, limped home with hardly any whales. Shortly afterwards negotiations between the two nations brought peace and they began whaling again in earnest, along with the Germans, French and Danes.

Having initially hired Basque whalers to teach them the tricks of the trade, the whaling crews sailed to Spitsbergen every summer as the midnight sun rose in the sky and thawed the impenetrable ice cover of winter. Their arrival coincided with the whales' feeding season, heralded by the appearance of the sun and subsequent explosion of marine life. During the summer a bowhead whale consumes 500–1500 kg (1100–3300 lb) of food daily, filtering innumerable tiny animals through its baleen.

It stockpiles energy as blubber to see it through the dark days of winter.

The whalers set up camps and tryworks on the beach and scanned the sea for the familiar rolling black backs and towering vapour plumes – twin 7 m (23 ft) high, v-shaped sprays produced by two widely spaced blowholes – of the bowhead whale. Like the Basques they hunted with hand-held harpoons, chasing the whales across treacherous ice-studded seas, at times battered by howling winds, blinded by soupy fogs and frozen by sub-zero temperatures.

Dead whales were towed to shore to be processed. The whalers stripped off the blubber, which they 'tried out' to release the oil, then hacked the baleen from the jaw and scrubbed off the gum tissue. The whalemen knew that the baleen had to be quickly and thoroughly cleaned before the tissue decomposed and developed an unpleasant smell that reduced its value. Except for a small amount of whale meat taken to supplement the whalers' meagre diet, the rest of the corpse was simply discarded, attracting mobs of raucous seabirds and scavenging polar bears. The whaling continued all summer until the sun lowered in the sky, the gloom of winter descended, and the ships headed home.

At first the Greenland fishery boomed. With a combination of aggressive economic ambition and unmatched practical efficiency, the Dutch defied the British to become the most successful whaling nation in the region. During the early years they accumulated such huge stocks of oil and baleen that cargo ships had to be sent out from Holland to transport the surplus home. The Dutch even established a semi-permanent settlement called Smeerenburg – 'Blubber Town' – on Spitsbergen's unwelcoming rocky shore. Unlike the average malodorous shore station, Smeerenburg was an authentic Dutch town boasting a church, a fort, shops and taverns. Enterprising tradesmen followed the whalers and supplied them with alcohol, tobacco, coffee and fresh bread.

But within a century the glory days of Greenland whaling were over. Having decimated the inshore bowheads the whalers had to travel out into the Arctic Ocean in pursuit of their prey, leaving the security of land behind. They flensed the carcasses either on ice floes or by harnessing them to the side of the ship in open water and stowed the blubber in barrels. Spitsbergen became deserted once more – the Smeerenburg traders shut up shop and the town, exposed to the full destructive force of the Arctic climate, soon disintegrated.

The whalers were now hunting their quarry within the pack ice, following open leads and dodging icebergs. Although a perilous place for humans to venture, this extreme environment is the realm of the bowhead whale, which is perfectly adapted to survive there. As well as its thickly enveloping coat of blubber the bowhead lacks a dorsal fin, which would impede its progress through the ice. It can dive for up to an hour – longer than any other baleen whale. The ability to remain submersed under pack ice is crucial, giving the whale sufficient time to find infrequently sited breathing holes. If no breathing hole exists the bowhead can use its powerful body and large head to ram its way through ice 50 cm (20 in) thick.

While the bowhead was in its element, the whalemen struggled like fish out of water. As the whales became scarcer they were forced to push into ever more remote and dangerous waters. Relying solely on wind power, the whalers were largely defenceless in their battle with the capricious Arctic climate. Ships frequently became trapped when unmerciful winds shifted the pack ice. Those that could not escape its clutches faced a long, dark, bitterly cold winter until the ice melted the following year. Anxious to keep costs down, most shipowners provisioned their ships with food to last only six months and stranded crews often perished through starvation.

By the late 18th century risks and losses far outweighed dwindling gains and the industry slumped. But while the Europeans were scouring Arctic waters for the last bowheads, a new industry had already been launched on the other side of the Atlantic. American whaling would soon dominate the world.

THE AMERICAN WHALING ENTERPRISE grew up around the ports of New England, especially the small island of Nantucket whose name became virtually synonymous with whaling. At first the colonists hunted only right whales that passed by close to shore. But in 1712 that all changed. According to a possibly apocryphal but popular story, a whaleship captained by one Christopher Hussey was blown out to sea during an unexpected storm. To their surprise the crew found themselves adrift amongst a school of sperm whales. Hussey was not a man to miss a golden opportunity. Despite the turbulent weather he ordered his men to kill one. The storm abated, they towed the carcass home, and an industry was born.

The locals were already aware of the existence of the sperm whale because a stranded individual had washed up on their beach 12 years earlier. But they had never known where the sperm whales lived, nor that they existed in such great numbers. What they did know, however, was that although the sperm whale had no baleen it yielded oil that fetched the very highest prices. By this time the local stocks of right whales had already started their inevitable decline. Inspired by the commercial potential of Hussey's discovery the whalers equipped their ships for longer voyages and headed out to the open ocean to seek their fortunes.

The sperm whale is the largest of all the toothed whales; females grow to 11 m (36 ft), while males can exceed 17 m (56 ft) in length. Eschewing shallow coastal waters the sperm whale is a true inhabitant of the deep sea and is found in all the oceans of the world. Its dark grey or black body, wrinkled like a prune in parts, is adorned with white lips and whitish spots on the belly. The sperm whale's unmistakeable blunt-angled head is enormous, occupying up to a third of the total body length. It contains the largest brain of any animal on Earth, weighing in at a ponderous 7.8 kg (17 lb) in mature males. Below this is a relatively small and thin lower jaw studded with fearsome cone-shaped teeth that fit into sockets in the upper jaw.

The sperm whale's diet consists of fish and squid, in pursuit of which it dives to extraordinary depths of up to 2 km (1¼ miles) or even 3 km (1¾ miles) – probably deeper than any other marine mammal. Most of the species it pursues are relatively small but occasionally a sperm whale will tackle a giant squid. Sucker marks on the bodies of some whales, inflicted by a squid's 10 m (33 ft) long tentacles, bear witness to titanic battles in the benthic gloom.

For most of the 18th century sperm whaling flourished. Ships set out from Nantucket and other New England ports, heading north and south. The ice-bound vessels entered the Davis Strait and Baffin Bay; those on a southerly course hugged the coast down to Brazil or crossed the Atlantic and scouted for whales around the Azores and Cape Verde islands and along the west coast of Africa to Namibia. By the 1770s voyages were extending the length of South America to the Falkland Islands and other lonely outposts in the South Atlantic. The shipbuilders were kept busy, frenetically producing new vessels to keep up with the burgeoning demand.

Initially the length of whaling voyages was kept in check by the necessity of returning to port to process the blubber. This issue was especially pertinent for those heading south, as the blubber would rapidly spoil in the heat of the tropical sun. The ingenious American whalers soon solved the problem. First they developed a portable tryworks that could be carried on board the ship. The crew would land on a convenient beach, set up the try-works, render the blubber and then carry on sailing. This was soon superseded by a second innovation – on-board tryworks. Once the blubber could be processed on deck, a vessel could stay at sea for months or even years until it had accumulated a full cargo of oil. After 1750 the average duration of a voyage jumped from six weeks to four months.

The New England oil boom suffered a serious setback during the American Wars of Independence, which began in 1775. The residents of Nantucket, being ardent Quakers and committed pacifists (at least when it came to the human species), did not participate in the fighting but they got caught in the crossfire between the two warring factions. At the end of the war their fleet had been reduced from 100 whaleships to 35. Undaunted, the whalers went straight back to business. Then in 1789 the industry was given a boost when the *Emilia*, an English vessel mastered by a Nantucketer, rounded Cape Horn and killed the first Pacific sperm whale off the coast of Chile. The Pacific pioneers had discovered a plentiful and as yet untapped supply of sperm whales. As whaling fever spread, vessels flocked to the Pacific to harvest its 'liquid gold'. In 1840 three-quarters of those vessels were American. The wealth they generated gave the fledgling republic's economy an important boost. The industry reached its peak in 1846, when 735 ships and over 70,000 people were engaged in the whale fishery. By this time the port of New Bedford had displaced Nantucket as the heart of the industry.

The whalers studied the whales and attempted to plot their movements. Sperm whales range throughout the tropics and warm temperate zones. Adult males travel to higher latitudes than females, braving the cold waters at the margins of the polar pack ice in their search for squid. On reaching the whaling grounds the whalers scoured the sea systematically and killed every whale they could find, males, females and calves alike. They took between 8000 and 10,000 whales every year. Once the whales had been eliminated from an area the whalers moved on in search of more. They gradually dispersed throughout the Pacific and rounded the Cape of Good Hope to crop the whales of the Indian Ocean. By this time most voyages were seafaring marathons lasting on average two to three years. Whaling had developed its own culture, rituals and language, immortalised in the classic works of Herman Melville.

The whaling ships were about 30 m (100 ft) long and sufficiently robust to survive being buffeted by a roiling sea while carrying a heavy cargo and with a whale lashed to one side. They were designed to withstand climatic extremes from polar ice to equatorial heat, and were spacious enough to accommodate several years' worth of provisions and supplies as well as a homebound cargo of 2000–3000 barrels of oil. Up in the crow's nest, 30 m (100 ft) above deck, lookouts worked on continuous two-hour shifts from sunrise to sunset, scanning the ocean for sperm whales. On days with clear visibility they could see up to 12 km (7 miles) away. An experienced hand had no problems identifying the unique and distinctive blow of the sperm whale. It projects forwards and to the left from the whale's single blowhole situated on the left-hand side at the very front of the head. Whalemen believed that the whales spouted a type of water so pungent and noxious that contact with the spray could cause mental disorders and sear the skin. Even Herman Melville wrote, "if the jet is fairly spouted into your eyes it will blind you".

The whalers were wrong on all counts. Although the blow might contain some trapped droplets, whales do not spout water. The blowhole is the equivalent of a land mammal's nostril and is the orifice through which they breathe air. Unlike land mammals, which breathe automatically, whales have developed conscious breathing to ensure they do not inhale while underwater. To inhale the whale flexes a muscle that opens the blowhole. As it prepares to submerge it relaxes the muscle and the blowhole clamps tightly shut. When the whale surfaces again it exhales explosively, releasing a blast of air. The water vapour in the air condenses creating the fine mist spotted by the lookouts.

On sighting a blow the lookout would cry out the whaler's alert: "There she blows!" Immediately the ship became a frenzy of activity as the crew prepared and launched the whaleboats. American whaleboats were typically made of cedar clapboard and pointed at both ends, like a modern canoe, so that they could be paddled in both directions. They were sleek, manoeuvrable vessels that could slip through the water at high speed. Equipped with a mast, sail and rudder, as well as oars and paddles, they could be sailed or rowed depending on the wind conditions. The boats each carried a crew of six: the 'boatheader' whose position was filled by either the captain or one of the mates, the harpooner and four oarsmen. They sped towards the whale as stealthily as possible so that the animal would not hear them and flee. The harpooner stood at the front while the boatheader stood at the rear and steered the boat. Everyone else had their backs towards the terrifying bulk of their prey, which was probably for the best. The boatheader aimed to approach the whale in a direct path to its head or tail flukes, staying out of its line of vision.

The harpoon consisted of a forged iron head mounted on a 4 m (13 ft) wooden shaft attached to the boat by a long coil of line. At the right moment, when the boatheader shouted "give it to him", the harpooner leapt into action, plunging the harpoon into the whale's back and embedding the head securely in the blubber. This was a critical moment: the whale might react by swimming away across the water, by diving down to the ocean depths, or by turning on the boat and smashing it with its head or tail, flinging the crew into the water. Most whales dived, causing the line attached to the harpoon to unravel so rapidly that it smoked with friction and needed dousing with sea water to prevent it burning. After failing to escape its tormentors underwater, the whale would usually re-surface and take off on the 'Nantucket sleigh-ride', bouncing the whaleboat along behind it at speeds of up to 30 km/h (18 mph). As the whale weakened, the crew slowly hauled themselves in along the line.

Meanwhile the boatheader and harpooner carefully changed positions so that the boatheader was at the front. When close enough, the boatheader raised a sharpened steel lance and plunged it into the whale. He aimed for the lungs, stabbing the whale behind the left flipper and probing through the thick blubber to find the animal's inner organs. He vigorously 'churned' the lance, piercing and ripping the tissue. Once he hit the right spot the whale's lungs filled with blood. Its spout transformed into a crimson mist that cascaded over the boat and drenched the men. With a cry of "there's fire in the chimney!" the crew knew that they had conquered their prey. They backed off and watched the huge beast go into the 'flurry'. Thrashing violently the whale swam in ever decreasing circles, crashing its tail into the water and regurgitating chunks of partly digested squid. Shuddering in its death throes, the whale finally fell silent and lay 'fin out' and unmoving in a slick of blood and vomit.

Despite having just risked life and limb to kill the whale the whalemen's work was only just beginning. First they had to transport their mighty prize back to the ship. If the winds were favourable they could erect the sail, but if not the weary crew had to row the boat towing the dead weight behind them. Once back at the ship the whale was secured to the side and a wooden platform – the 'cutting stage' – was placed on top of it. A seaman equipped with long-handled knives and sharp spades was then lowered down to the platform on a rope. It was important to process the whale quickly before the snapping sharks that encircled it had devoured too much of the valuable carcass. First the head was cut off and left to float while the blubber was stripped in a spiral sheet like the peeling of an orange. The strips were cut into large 'blanket pieces', forked onto the deck and stowed below decks in the 'blubber room'. Next the head was brought aboard. The sperm whale's cavernous head contains spermaceti – the finest and most valuable of all whale oils. It was the desire for spermaceti that to a great extent fuelled the massive sperm-whaling industry.

Spermaceti means 'seed of the whale'. The whale was named far back in history when observers mistakenly assumed that it stored its sperm in its head. Spermaceti is liquid at body temperature but solidifies to a whitish wax, like soft paraffin, when exposed to cooler air. Its primary function in the whale is to focus sound waves, channelling the animal's characteristic clicking noises, although it may also serve other purposes. The whalers slashed open the 'case', an elongated barrel-shaped organ in the upper part of the head, to reveal a reservoir of soft, white, spongy tissue saturated with spermaceti. They also collected the precious oil from the lower part of the head, the 'junk', where it is held in a matrix of tough fibres. The oil was bailed into casks and the remains of the head thrown to the ravening sharks. Spermaceti

Spermaceti being factory processed in 1901.

was valuable because it was used to make the highest quality candles that burned brightly and cleanly without producing smoke or odour. Some people believed it also had medicinal properties and could successfully relieve the effects of renal colic and pulmonary ulcers. It later became a sought-after lubricant.

After the spermaceti had been stowed the blubber was tried-out. The on-board tryworks consisted of two 900 litre (200 gallon) cauldrons set over a furnace and surrounded by a protective brick perimeter. The pots stood in a tray of seawater to prevent the deck from scorching and catching fire. The whalers hauled blanket pieces up from the blubber room and cut them into smaller chunks, known as 'horse pieces', using two-handled knives. They deeply scored the horse pieces, which were then referred to as 'bible leaves' because they resembled the fanned pages of a book. The bible leaves were cooked in the cauldrons and the oil was piped into casks for storage.

Although sperm whale oil was not as valuable as spermaceti oil it was still superior to the oil of other species. While sperm whale oil was a light straw colour, the oil from other whales was brown, the shade varying according to the age and general health of the animal. American whaling merchants sometimes instructed ship captains that "brown oil is better than no oil" – if sperm whales could not be captured the captain was to pursue other species rather than return home without a full cargo. Right whales, found in various parts of the Atlantic and Pacific Oceans, were still a popular target because they supplied great quantities of oil as well as valuable baleen.

Sperm whale oil was a superb illuminant and was burned in the finest lamps. Later the discovery that it retains its lubricating qualities in extreme temperatures created a great demand from a number of industries. It was used in the manufacture of such diverse commodities as watch oil, hydraulic fluids, lubricant for delicate high-altitude instruments, glycerine for explosives, cosmetics ("imparts a rich glossy sheen"), luxury soap, rust-proofing compounds, detergent, margarine, vitamins, glaze on photographs, over 70 pharmaceutical compounds and typewriter ribbons.

The sperm whale occasionally rewarded the whalers with the most desirable product of all: ambergris. This waxy substance occurs in the intestines of only 1–5% of sperm whales. Chancing upon it was a cause for celebration since it was literally worth its weight in gold. Lumps of ambergris usually have an irregular roundish shape like a potato. Dark chocolaty brown on the outside and pale yellow to light grey on the inside, ambergris has the consistency of dry clay. Each lump can weigh 0.1–10 kg (¼–22 lb), but very occasionally giant boulders of ambergris are recovered. The largest on record, weighing a staggering 420 kg (926 lb), was removed from a 15 m (50 ft) bull sperm whale killed in the Southern Ocean in 1953. When first retrieved

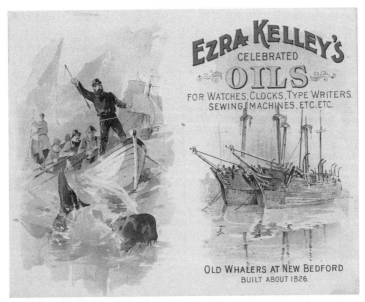

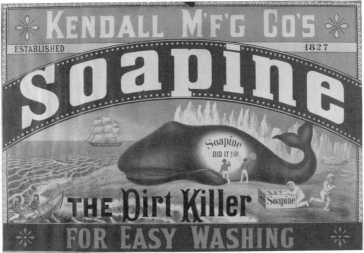

Sperm whale oil was of the best quality and had an enormous variety of uses (top). In the 19th century Soapine, a household soap, was one of the best-known brands in the USA (bottom).

ambergris smells strongly of its origins, but after a while the offensive odour fades to an earthy, musky aroma. The cause of its production has never been verified, but it is known to consist primarily of ambrein, a fatty substance similar to cholesterol, and it is always studded with undigested squid beaks. Ambergris is occasionally found floating in the sea or washed ashore, having been excreted by a whale. From as early as the ninth century it was highly prized throughout the Muslim world as a spice, aphrodisiac, incense, laxative and medicine. But its origins had remained a mystery until the American sperm whalers found it lodged in the guts of their prey. Thereafter it became invaluable as a fixative in perfumes and fetched tremendous prices until it was replaced by synthetics in the 20th century.

The whalemen continued the mammoth task of processing the whale round the clock, working alternating six-hour shifts until the last barrel of oil was in the hold. If more than one whale had been caught this could take several days. It was foul and dangerous work – crew members could be crushed by the enormous weight of strips of blubber, wounded by assorted sharp, unwieldy knives, or splashed with boiling oil. The deck became so slippery with blood and oil that people sometimes skidded overboard and fell into the shark-infested sea. When they eventually finished, both the men and their ship would be caked with grease, blood and soot. The final task was a massive clean-up, during which they did their best to scrape off the indelible stench of boiled blubber that seemed to impregnate every pore. At last the crew laid down their tools and rested until the cry of the lookout rang out over the ship, and all hands leapt on deck once again.

A whaleship typically left port with a crew of 30–35 men. The captain and his mates lived in relative luxury near the stern of the vessel while the harpooners and coopers were lodged towards the centre in rooms that were less well-appointed but still comfortable.

Down near the bow the ordinary seamen lived, slept and ate in one cramped, dark and filthy communal room that swarmed with cockroaches, bedbugs and rats. The food was equally revolting. Despite being available in abundance, whale meat was rarely eaten because the taste was considered unpleasant. But the alternatives were hardly tempting – while the officers enjoyed fresh bread, butter and sugar, the majority of the crew ate a basic diet of salted pork, beef or horse, and thick, hard crackers. Ben Ezra Stiles Ely, who embarked on a whaling voyage at the tender age of 17, later wrote a colourful account of his gastronomic experiences on board:

"... no swine that gleans the gutters ever subsisted on viler meat and bread than did our crew. It may seem incredible, but it is nevertheless true, that our beef and pork in general would produce a stench from the stem to the stern of the vessel, whenever a barrel was opened. It was old and partially decayed meat. Much of it was green and putrid. Not a little of our bread was so infested with vermin, that after having crumbled it into hot water and molasses, which was called coffee, I could skim the worms and weavels off with my spoon."

Life consisted of long periods of utmost tedium punctuated by spells of terrifying danger and extreme exertion. Records disclose a huge variety of unexpected dramas including castaways, mutinies, desertions, floggings, women stowaways, drunkenness, scurvy, fever, collisions, fire at sea, drownings, hurricanes, earthquakes, tidal waves, lightning strikes, hostile natives, men falling from the masthead and ships crushed by ice. One of the scariest potential mishaps was a whale that decided to retaliate. Most sperm whales are docile and timid, but mature males can be pugnacious. Although they rarely launched deliberate attacks, the possibility that fuelled the young Melville's imagination remained a constant source of fear for the whalers. The clue to their behaviour lies in the complex organisation of sperm whale society. Male and female sperm whales have very different life histories. Females usually spend their entire lives with other females in 'nursery schools' along with their calves and immature adults of both sexes. Males leave their mothers between the ages of four and 15 and form loose associations called 'bachelor schools'. As they mature other males become rivals rather than allies. They sometimes engage in vicious fights over access to reproductive females, locking jaws, wrestling and biting each other's heads. Given this occasional tendency to belligerence and experience of combat, it is no surprise that enraged sperm whales sometimes turned on the boats, lunging at them with teeth bared and using their enormous, cushioned heads as battering rams.

During the early years of the sperm-whaling industry many young men, enticed by visions of exotic destinations, dusky maidens and handsome financial rewards, willingly signed up to work on a whaleship. But once on board their romantic dreams were soon shattered by the reality of their situation. As well as the physical privations and constant threat of danger, the earnings they anticipated often failed to materialise. Although there were fortunes to be made, they rarely filtered down to the lower ranks. Profits were shared and everyone received a percentage of the value of the cargo. This 'lay system' had originated in Nantucket to ensure a fair distribution of proceeds. But as the industry grew, the economic structure that had once underpinned small community enterprises became simply another way to exploit the workers. Ordinary seamen received about 0.6% of the take and lowly cabin boys as little as 0.3%. As working conditions deteriorated ship owners found it increasingly hard to assemble crews. In desperation they hired the services of unscrupulous shipping agents. These 'landsharks', as they were popularly known, lured gullible

Casks of whale oil await distribution on New Bedford wharf, 1870.

young men into taverns and plied them with rum. The following day the victim would struggle awake to find himself aboard a whaleship that had already set sail. He would have months or even years to repent his naivety. Unsurprisingly, desertion was rife.

In the second half of the 19th century a number of circumstances conspired to bring an end to New England's whaling supremacy. During the American Civil War, which raged from 1861 to 1865, confederate raiders captured and burned many whaling ships. On previous occasions such destruction had caused only a glitch in the inexorable expansion of the industry, but this time whaling could not recover. There were far fewer whales to be found – even the seemingly endless depths of the Pacific were becoming fished out. Another key factor was the rise of petroleum, first discovered and pumped out of the ground in Pennsylvania in 1859. When kerosene, extracted from petroleum, was introduced as a cheap lighting fuel it began to push the price of whale oil down.

By the time the New Englanders put their whaling days behind them the hub of the American whaling industry had relocated to San Francisco on the other side of the continent. From here the whalers could more easily exploit the remaining sperm whales in the Pacific as well as satisfying the continuing demand for whalebone by hunting right whales, bowheads, humpbacks and gray whales.

AMERICA WAS NOT THE ONLY colony whose economy was given a helping hand by the providential existence of whales offshore. For the first half of the 19th century settlers in Australia, New Zealand and South Africa were all delighted to discover right whales cavorting near their coastlines. These were southern right whales, close relatives of the northern species that had initially prompted the growth of commercial whaling. Almost identical to its northern counterpart, the southern right whale passes the austral summer in the remote reaches of the Antarctic Ocean where it feasts on vast blooms of tiny plankton. During the cold winter months it migrates north and congregates in shallow bays and estuaries to mate and deliver calves. For millennia these bays had provided warm water and security from the dangers of the open ocean. Now they harboured hunters.

The right whales abounded in such numbers that the whalers thought their luck would never run out. In Tasmania's Derwent Estuary the herds were so dense that it was hard to navigate small boats through them, while one visitor in Wellington Harbour complained that the whales kept him awake all night with the noise of their mating antics. Once so accessible to hunters because of its preference for inshore waters, the southern right whale is now the easiest whale for scientists to study and unusual amounts of information have been gleaned about these sexual activities. While wintering in the bays, sexually receptive females mate with a number of males. Males cruise around looking for suitable partners and if a female is already engaged, the next male will generally wait his turn patiently. Unlike sperm whales, right whales never compete for females with physical violence. But they do compete after copulation has been completed – with their sperm. Each male produces copious quantities of sperm with which he tries to flush out his predecessor's deposit in the female's vaginal passage. To produce the necessary volume, male southern right whales have the largest testes in the animal kingdom, each one weighing an impressive 500 kg (1102 lb). They also have extra-long penises – over 2.5 m (8 ft) in length – to help them gain a competitive edge.

A year later the female will give birth to the victor's 6 m (20 ft) long offspring. Mothers form strong bonds with their calves and the whalers were quick to take advantage of this. They knew that if they wounded a calf its mother would not abandon it, even as she was being killed herself. By targeting females and their calves the whalers rapidly eradicated the once huge southern right whale herds, and their own source of income.

IN 1935 RIGHT WHALES became the first whales to receive international protection. Since then the southern right whale has been slowly recovering, despite illegal whaling by the Soviet Union until the 1970s. The population is fairly stable, although it numbers no more than 7000. Its northern cousins have not fared so well and their future is in jeopardy. In the North Atlantic a remnant population off the east coast of North America hovers at around 300.

It is thought that even fewer right whales now inhabit the North Pacific. Their population was almost completely annihilated by the zealous Americans and denied the opportunity to recover by illegal Soviet whaling in the 20th century. An exceptionally slow breeding rate hampers their revival – females typically bear a single calf once every three to five years. The North Pacific population is so small that any calves produced could suffer from the effects of inbreeding. The bowheads of Spitsbergen have similarly failed to bounce back. Although larger herds exist elsewhere, the Spitsbergen population now numbers only in the tens. Before the whalers arrived there may have been as many as 24,000 of these gentle giants.

Of all the whales targeted during the early history of whaling – right whales, the bowhead whale, and the sperm whale – only the sperm whale is not seriously endangered. There are thought to be 360,000 globally, although pre-whaling estimates suggest that between 1.5 and 2 million once roamed the world's oceans. American whalers kept detailed accounts, but the information they provide is imprecise. The whalers did not count the number of whales they killed, but instead registered the barrels of oil and pounds of baleen delivered at the home port. Furthermore, some of the haul was not recorded. Carcasses that sank, whale products traded for goods at ports of call, and calves that starved after their mothers were killed have all been erased from history.

Armed and dangerous

On industrial-scale whaling

Whaling technology remained largely unchanged for over 800 years. Whaling ships navigated the oceans under sail. On finding whales they dispatched small wooden boats that were also driven by the wind, if weather conditions were obliging, or by muscle power. When the crew reached their quarry they secured it with hand-thrown harpoons and stabbed it to death with long lances. The whalers were enormously successful in their pursuit of certain species but with their homespun equipment there remained a number of whales that they simply could not catch and kill.

During the vibrant years of the late 19th century the entrepreneurs of the Industrial Revolution generated a plethora of innovations and inventions. Whaling, along with many other industries, modernised dramatically. The whalers acquired steam-powered ships and superior weaponry. Their new arsenal removed all limitations – they could now travel wherever they wanted and kill whichever whales they found there. Luck no longer played a part; instead a whale was almost certainly doomed from the moment it was sighted by the lookout. And more importantly for crew members, they no longer gambled with their lives for the sake of the hunt. In the 20th century, as technology continued to improve and new markets for whale products opened up, whales were killed in staggering numbers. The free-for-all did eventually become subject to regulation but only after many of the world's largest animals had been driven to the very brink of extinction.

By the early 19th century whalers were becoming frustrated with the limited range of hand-held harpoons. Then in 1837 William Greener, an English gunsmith with a reputation for creative thinking, came to their rescue. His landmark invention, the Greener Gun, could shoot a harpoon further and with much greater force than any human. The gun was mounted in

THE WHALE FISHERY.

Boat fastened to whale by harpoon and line; killing the whale with bomb-lances.   (Sect. v, vol. ii, pp. 45, 262, 267.)

From painting by J. S. Ryder.

Attached to the boat by a harpoon line, this whale cannot escape the deadly bomb lance.

the bow of the whaleboat and could be swivelled to aim at the whale. It became immensely popular despite a major flaw – the massive recoil it produced frequently damaged the insubstantial boats.

In 1846 gun manufacturers optimistically announced a solution to the problem. They had devised a gun that could be fired from a man's shoulder rather than a swivel. In practice, however, the shoulder gun was a far from perfect remedy. It discharged slender harpoons which, encumbered by the heavy trailing whale line, did not fly straight and often missed their target. And despite firing lightweight missiles, the gun still produced a powerful recoil that hurled a number of gunners backwards overboard and shattered the collarbones of many others.

But while the shoulder gun was not entirely effective with harpoons it proved deadly in firing the bomb lance. Designed to replace the hand lance, the bomb lance was a rocket-shaped metal cylinder equipped with an internal time fuse. When the gun was fired, gunpowder sparked and ignited the fuse. The lance embedded in the whale, the fuse burnt down, and the bomb detonated. The explosion shredded the whale's insides either mortally wounding or killing it outright. The onslaught had just stepped up a gear.

FOR MOST OF THE 18TH AND 19TH centuries, while the Americans were gainfully occupied hunting the sperm whale, British whalers continued their pursuit of the bowhead. From Spitsbergen, where they founded the industry in the 17th century, they moved westward gradually expanding throughout the eastern Arctic. In 1817, having rounded Greenland and successfully navigated the ice-strewn waters of the Davis Strait, they forced a passage through to Baffin Bay.

Although home to huge, undisturbed herds of bowheads, Baffin Bay was an extremely hazardous environment to work in. Negotiating the ice in wind-powered vessels, the whalemen were tormented by the mercurial polar climate. Howling winds caused the pack ice to shift unpredictably, trapping and crushing their ships. Parsimonious ship owners did not budget for over-wintering so any whaler whose ship was immobilised faced at best months of misery and at worst death from a combination of exposure and every sailor's *bête noire*, scurvy. In Baffin Bay the British had reached their limits. They were unaware of the existence of the western Arctic bowheads, but even if they had known they could not have traversed the perilous seas north of Canada to reach them.

By the time the American Pacific fleet discovered the bow-heads of the western Arctic, the industry was undergoing profound changes. Unlike the British, the Americans came armed with sophisticated weapons and they were much better equipped to meet the challenges of the polar environment. The Americans were venturing north in response to a changing market. In the second half of the 19th century the price of whale oil tumbled and the value of baleen skyrocketed. A huge demand was created by the women's clothing industry as hand-span waists and full flaring skirts became a fashion staple. Strong and bendable, 'whalebone' was the perfect material for the corsets and hoops necessary to mould the human body into improbable forms. Sperm whales did not yield any baleen and were becoming increasingly scarce so the whalers set off to find baleen-rich right whales.

A forest of whalebone from the Arctic drying in San Francisco.

The American whalemen had never seen a bowhead so they had no idea that a whale yielding even greater quantities of precious baleen existed. The first bowheads they encountered were in the Okhotsk Sea, an almost circular body of water bounded by Siberia to the north and divided from the Bering Sea by the volcano-studded Kamchatka Peninsula to the east. Within a few years the Okhotsk bowheads had been virtually eliminated. Meanwhile the hunt for fresh stocks continued. In 1848 the *Superior* sailed through the Bering Sea, breached the Bering Strait, and emerged into the Arctic Ocean. Here the whalers found bowheads in numbers that exceeded all their expectations. Their discovery precipitated a stampede as whaleships rushed to the western Arctic to share in the bonanza.

The whalers' novel weapons were instrumental to their success. The swivel gun with its long-range capability allowed them to shoot from a distance. The bomb lance, by striking a rapid death blow, prevented struck whales from taking refuge under the ice. By the early 1880s the whalers had converted to steam power enabling their vessels to thrust deeper into the Arctic to access ever more remote hunting grounds. In 1889 the fleet entered the Beaufort Sea and found the world's last pristine stock of bowhead whales. With baleen now the only valuable part of the carcass the whalers simply cut it out and discarded the rest of the whale.

By the end of the century the industry was fizzling out. The American Civil War and a series of shipping disasters took their toll but ultimately the whalers had to give up because there were no more whales left to kill. The industries that utilised baleen responded to its insufficient supply by turning to spring steel as a cheaper and more reliable substitute, and by the first decade of the 20th century the baleen market had collapsed.

The international community banned the commercial killing of bowheads in 1931. But by this time just a fraction of the herd that once roamed the northern ice remained. Fortunately some populations are now showing encouraging signs of recovery. About 10,000 bowhead whales migrate between the Bering, Chukchi and Beaufort Seas. The Davis Strait-Baffin Bay population, almost completely destroyed by the British, now numbers about 8000 whales. Other populations are not faring so well, however. In the Okhotsk Sea only 150–200 bowheads cling onto existence by the narrowest of margins.

THE IMPROVED TECHNOLOGY of the 19th century facilitated another industry that was even more intense and short-lived. This targeted the most obstreperous of cetaceans – the gray whale. Until then the gray whale, a mysticete, had never been a popular quarry. Its oil was of poor quality compared with that of the sperm whale and it did not yield huge quantities like the right and bowhead whales. The baleen, which is creamy-white to pale yellow in colour, short in length and coarse in texture, was not commercially viable. Furthermore, the gray whale had a vicious temper – the whalers called it 'devilfish' because of its tendency to fight to the bitter end. But, inevitably, as numbers of other species plummeted, this great mottled beast gradually became a more attractive prey.

The gray whale differs from its fellow mysticetes in various ways. Instead of scooping prey from the water, it feeds on the sea bed by rolling to one side, sweeping its head along the floor, and sucking sediment into its mouth. The sediment contains abundant small creatures – crustaceans and other invertebrates – which are filtered out by the baleen. The whale swallows them and surfaces with plumes of sand and mud flowing from its mouth. Most gray whales feed by rolling to the right but a few are 'left-handed' feeders.

The gray whale does most of its feeding in the Arctic from May to October. Throughout the summer it eats almost continuously, replenishing its reserves and storing up fat to see it through the lean months of winter. As autumn chills the air and the days shorten it heads south. Its destination is Baja California, the narrow sun-baked peninsula that extends like a crooked finger into the Pacific Ocean alongside the mainland of Mexico. Its

CALIFORNIA GRAYS AMONG THE ICE

A NORTHERN WHALING SCENE.

After his retirement from whaling, Charles Scammon travelled to Alaska and drew the gray whales there (top). Whaling off the northwest coast of the USA, as depicted by Charles Scammon in 1874 (bottom).

10,000 km (6000 mile) journey takes about three months. Arriving in late December the whales head for the warm, shallow lagoons that scallop the peninsula. The pregnant females enter the lagoons to deliver and nurse calves conceived a year earlier. They seek quiet corners, escaping the rowdy activities of males and juveniles, which patrol to and fro seeking mates, courting, playing and socialising. In the lagoons, the gray whales are visited by shimmering silver fish called topsmelt. The gray whale is encrusted with more parasites than any other cetacean, with 100–200 kg (220–440 lb) of barnacles attached to its head and body, and thousands of whale lice that cluster in skin folds and swarm into wounds. The topsmelt groom the whales, feasting on the protein-rich parasites and the whales' old, flaky skin.

American sperm whalers first encountered gray whales in 1846 in Bahia Magdalena, a complex of protected bays towards the southern tip of the peninsula. They depleted these stocks but never found where the rest of the whales were hiding. Then in 1856 Charles Scammon arrived. Scammon was the first whaler with real ambitions for gray whale hunting. He realised that despite the inferior quality of the whale's tea-coloured oil, he would be able to accrue a full cargo in just a single season if he could find a large enough concentration of animals. Scammon went in search of the whales' breeding sanctuaries and in 1858 he struck gold. He discovered the Laguna Ojo de Liebre, the most northerly and important of the Baja California nurseries. Soon to become known as Scammon's Lagoon, this body of shallow water thronged with females and newborns – the whalemen could hardly navigate their boats for bumping into whales.

The moment he started turning his vision into reality, Scammon learned why the gray whale had received its fearsome moniker. The animals reacted to assault with unmatched ferocity, lashing out with their flukes, ramming boats and tangling harpoon lines. Their counterattacks created gruesome battlescenes — the water churned into a lather reddened with the blood of both sides. During the first major skirmish half the crew sustained injuries ranging from severe bruising to broken bones. Scammon waited a few days and then mounted a second attack. He assumed that his oarsmen had regained their courage, but when their boat closed on a whale they all panicked and leapt overboard. Scammon reported:

"... there is upsetting or staving of boats, the crew receiving bruises, cuts and, in many instances, having limbs broken; and repeated accidents have happened in which men have been instantly killed or received mortal injury."

Unwilling to abandon the hunt, the resourceful Scammon reconsidered his ammunition. He hit upon the idea of doing away with harpoons and simply killing the whales with bomb lances fired from harpoon guns. The whalers ambushed their prey from boats and blasted them with bombs until they died. Scammon knew that the success of his endeavour hinged on the weapons he used:

"... were it not for the utility of Greener's gun the coast fishery would be abandoned, it being now next to impossible to 'strike' with the hand-harpoon. At the present time, if the whale can be approached within thirty yards, it is considered to be in reach of the gun-harpoon."

The whalers accumulated so much oil that, having used all their barrels, they filled their bread casks, mincing tubs, coolers and trypots for the triumphant journey home. The following year Scammon went back and located the last of the gray whale's sanctuaries – the Laguna San Ignacio. By now word had spread and a small armada of expectant whalers accompanied him. An orgy of killing ensued. A favoured method was to harpoon a newborn calf and drag it ashore. Gray whale mothers bond closely with their calves; they stay close and stroke them with their flippers affectionately. As the cows instinctively tried to rescue their struggling offspring the whalers shot them from the shallows. Some whalers anchored outside the mouth of the lagoon and picked off animals that swam in and out, while others established shore stations along the Californian coast to intercept the whales on their epic migration.

By the 1870s over 8000 animals, excluding orphaned calves, had been killed and the industry was winding down. Because the whalemen had targeted females and calves the gray whale stocks had been decimated with unusual speed. It is not known whether Scammon was troubled by his conscience, but he certainly understood the consequences of his actions:

… "the large bays and lagoons, where these animals once congregated, brought forth and nurtured their young, are already nearly deserted. The mammoth bones of the California Gray lie bleaching on the shores of those silvery waters, and are scattered along the broken coasts, from Siberia to the Gulf of California; and ere long it may be questioned whether this mammal will not be numbered among the extinct species of the Pacific."

Historically there were three distinct populations of gray whale. A group in the North Atlantic became extinct, probably at the hands of whalers, by 1750. In the western Pacific another population, which was intensively hunted by the Japanese, Koreans and Russians in the 20th century, is critically endangered. The survivors number no more than a few hundred individuals and very little is known about them. The population in the eastern Pacific, which formed the basis for the Baja California industry, has conversely made a remarkable recovery. Having received protection from commercial hunting in 1946, at least 26,000 whales now make the yearly pilgrimage from the Arctic to the tropics. Their coastal migration route, which once made them such easy prey for hunters, is now the focus of a thriving whale-watching industry.

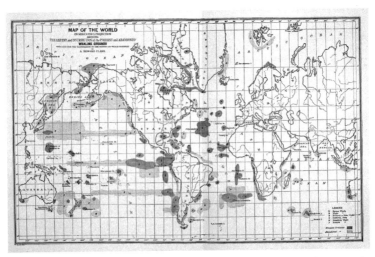

The world's whaling grounds in 1880. Dark shaded areas represent whaling grounds open at that time; lighter, dotted areas are those which had already been abandoned.

In 1868 a Norwegian whaler by the name of Svend Foyn went to sea in a whaleship quite unlike any other that had come before. The maiden voyage of the *Spes et Fides* marked the beginning of the age of modern whaling. By the second half of the 19th century the global whaling industry was stagnating. Almost all the known stocks of right whales, bowheads and sperm whales were commercially exhausted. Foyn at this time worked as a sealer. While out sealing he had seen other whales – giant creatures that nonchalantly cruised the icy waters of the North Atlantic, eluding the desperate whalers. When profits from the seal hunt shrank in the early 1860s Foyn set his sights on a much greater prize.

The whales he had observed off the shores of northern Norway were rorquals. The rorquals are a family of baleen whales whose intriguing name, meaning 'furrow' in Norwegian, refers to the parallel grooves that extend along the animal's throat and belly. As a rorqual opens its mouth to feed the furrows expand like the pleats of an accordion, allowing the whale to take enormous gulps of water. Of all the rorquals – the blue, fin, sei, Bryde's, minke and humpback whales – only the slow-moving humpback could occasionally be caught from a rowed whaleboat. The other species are swift swimmers and could easily outdistance the strongest of crews.

Cetaceans inherited their basic swimming action from their distant terrestrial ancestors. Like a galloping land mammal they flex the body up and down to propel themselves forwards. But while land animals move their limbs, a whale's tail flukes, powered by robust muscles above and below the spine, provide thrust. Their flippers act like flexible wings, allowing them to 'fly' through the water with great control.

Of all the great whales, rorquals are the fastest swimmers. Their long, tapered bodies are comparatively streamlined, minimising drag as they slip through the water. Unlike the more rotund right and bowhead whales, the rorquals are encased by a blubber sheath less than 30 cm (12 in) thick. The largest rorquals – the blue and fin whales – are also the fastest. Normal cruising speed is 10–20 km/h (6–12 mph), but when alarmed they are capable of bursts of 48 km/h (30 mph). For millennia the rorquals' unrivalled swimming prowess had kept them safe from capture as they roamed the world's oceans. On the odd occasion that a whaling crew did snare one, the carcass would usually sink before they could retrieve it.

For Foyn the rorquals' elusiveness was insupportable. A fervent Christian, he believed that God had endowed man with dominion over all other creatures. His mission was to exercise it over these ones. Foyn turned to technology to carry out his calling. His first innovation was the *Spes et Fides* (meaning *Hope and Faith*, both qualities that Foyn had in abundance). Steam-driven whaleships had already been adopted by the industry, but the whalemen still pursued their quarry in rowing boats. The *Spes et Fides* combined the function of whaleship and catcher boat in one sleek, speedy, highly manoeuvrable, steam-powered vessel.

Foyn also applied his genius to the whalers' arsenal. He fashioned a robust cannon that could be mounted on a swivel in the bow of the boat to replace the flimsy harpoon gun. The cannon could fire a harpoon 30–40 m (100–130 ft) and was sufficiently solid to absorb the recoil. Foyn's harpoons were also deadlier than their predecessors. They incorporated a grenade screwed to the tip and steel barbs that sprung open on impact, embedding the harpoon in the whale's flesh. Seconds later the grenade exploded, blasting a large hole and peppering the animal's insides with shrapnel.

Foyn used a hefty whale line and installed a steam-powered winch so that if the dead whale sank its carcass could by hauled up from the sea floor. By the summer of 1868 he was ready to trial his new system. On his first expedition he killed 30 rorquals. Learning from experience Foyn kept tinkering and improving his equipment. He added rollers and springs to absorb the stresses of the struggling whale and developed a compressor that pumped air into the animal's abdomen so that the carcass would not sink. Foyn had put whaling on a new course and so the annihilation of the world's largest animals began.

Foyn's countrymen were quick to grasp the superiority of his methods. Norwegian whaling began to spread like wildfire as the steam-driven catcher boats fanned out around the world in search of large whales to kill. Having devastated stocks in the Atlantic and Pacific Oceans all the way down to the southern coast of Africa, the Norwegians eventually arrived at the final frontier: Antarctica. Here in the remotest and most inaccessible place on Earth they found more rorqual whales than they could ever have imagined.

The rorquals were there in such numbers because of an abundance of their prey. In the Southern Ocean, icy polar waters from the south meet and merge with warmer currents from the north. These oceanic fronts, combined with the presence of sea ice, create special conditions in which the water has a high concentration of nutrients. In spring, when the ice melts and the water below absorbs life-giving sunlight, multitudes of microscopic plants bloom. The plants are the first link in a food chain that in just a couple of steps stretches all the way up to the great whales. The system hinges on an animal of diminutive size but infinite importance – krill.

Just 4 cm (1½ in) long, with bulbous black eyes facing forward like headlamps, and a translucent body encased by a glassy, red-tinged shell, krill look like tiny extraterrestrials. Their ten feathery legs paddle ceaselessly as they graze on microscopic plants near the water's surface. There are about 500 million tonnes of krill in the Southern Ocean, making it one of the most abundant animals on the planet. They are mostly found in small, scattered patches, but sometimes they aggregate in vast swarms stretching for kilometres in every direction and colouring the water orangey-red. Krill are the cornerstone of life in the Antarctic with most of the larger animals, including fish, squid, seabirds, seals and whales, dependent on them either directly or indirectly. They make up most of the diet of the rorqual whales, which devour them in extraordinary quantities. During the summer a blue whale consumes up to 40 million krill every day.

The small, shrimp-like crustaceans called krill are critically important to the Antarctic food chain.

FOLLOWING IN FOYN'S FOOTSTEPS, the next whaling pioneer was another Norwegian, Carl Anton Larsen. In 1903 Larsen captained an exploratory voyage to the Antarctic. He noted the pristine stocks of great whales and identified a suitable spot for a whaling station. His chosen location was South Georgia, a desolate island shaped like an eyebrow at the southern edge of the Atlantic. Back in Norway he outfitted an expedition and in 1904 returned to South Georgia where he established a temporary shore station in a sheltered harbour on the north coast. Larsen named the harbour Grytviken, or 'Cauldron Bay', after the boiling pots abandoned by sealers who had butchered the plump fur and elephant seals they found sprawling on its shores.

Larsen's enterprise was a triumph. In their first season his crew killed 195 whales, most of them humpbacks. Humpback whales were easy targets because they are slower than the other rorquals and migrate close to land in large pods of up to 15 animals. Humpbacks differ in various aspects of their anatomy, too. Unlike the classic rorquals, with their slim sleek bodies, the humpback is a bulky beast. Its knobbly skin is caked with barnacles and its cumbersome head is studded with bristle-sprouting protuberances called tubercles. Named for the way it arches its back out of the water to dive, the humpback's most distinctive features are its disproportionately long flippers; at 5 m (16 ft) they are the longest appendage of any animal in the world.

During the early years of the Antarctic industry humpbacks were the favoured prey. There were many more whales than a single shore station could process so others were built along South Georgia's north shore. But despite offering all the requisite elements for the construction of whale factories, South Georgia

Grytviken whaling station, South Georgia.

was an extremely inhospitable place. Its centre was a jumble of soaring, ice-clad mountains, its coastline scored with sheer-walled fjords plugged with ice that surged down from the glaciers above. There were no trees and very few plants. Subject to gale-force winds and temperatures far below zero, this was an unearthly landscape of ice and bare, unforgiving rock. Here grotesque machines broke giant bodies apart and the stench of death overwhelmed the senses. F.D. Ommanney, a scientist who visited South Georgia in 1929, described the apocalyptic scene:

"Flesh and guts lay about like small hillocks and blood flowed in rivers amid the racket of the winches and the thrashing of the rotary knife that sliced the blubber. Steel wires whipped and tautened in all directions while clouds of steam from winches and boilers arose as from a giant cauldron."

Despite the privations of life at the end of the world, Larsen's success prompted imitation. More and more catcher boats streamed south and shore stations were established on the Kerguelen Islands, the South Orkneys and the South Shetlands. The whalers found the humpbacks so easy to capture that they squandered the carcasses, maximising production by stripping off only the thickest most oil-rich blubber and discarding the rest. The British, who controlled most of the shore whaling areas, were both alarmed at the waste and keen to share in the profits. In 1911 they instituted a licensing system and started levying taxes. They also restricted the number of stations and catcher boats that could operate, prohibited the killing of females with calves, and required that the entire carcass be utilised.

The Norwegians responded by outfitting their cargo ships with blubber pots. Like the American sperm whalers, they could now flense the whales on platforms alongside the ships and render the blubber on board. The 'floating factories' were unable to operate in a turbulent sea and so were confined to sheltered bays and harbours, but by eschewing the land the Norwegians were exempt from British rules and regulations and could whale without restraint. The industry exterminated the local whale stocks with startling efficiency. By 1915 over 18,000 South Georgia humpbacks had been killed and the population was commercially extinct. By 1918 the humpbacks of the other islands had been wiped out, too. The hunters then turned their attention to another species – the blue whale.

The blue whale is an animal of implausible size and seemingly endless superlatives. It is not only the largest animal in the world; it is the largest that has ever lived. Up to 30 m (100 ft) in length, a blue whale can weigh in excess of 150 tonnes – heavier than 25 adult male African elephants. Its heart is the size of a small car; a human could crawl down its major arteries; 50 people could stand on its 3.8 tonne tongue. Baby blue whales have their own set of record-breaking statistics. A newborn is already 7 m (23 ft)

Called 'sulphurbottoms' by early Antarctic whalers, blue whales were a prize catch on account of their size.

long and weighs up to three tonnes. In the first year of its life a calf drinks 190 litres (330 pints) of milk daily, piling on about 3.6 kg (8 lb) of weight an hour or 90 kg (200 lb) a day.

The blue whale is so-called because it usually appears a luminous blue underwater. The Antarctic whalers, however, referred to it as a 'sulphurbottom' because in polar waters the skin attracts a coating of microscopic algae and takes on a yellow-brown tinge. Although they sometimes gather in large groups, blue whales usually feed alone or in pairs. Blue whales were highly prized by whalers simply because they were so big and yielded such a huge quantity of oil. Fast swimmers, living out in the deep ocean, they eluded the hunters until the invention of a new, crucial piece of technology. Conceived by yet another trail-blazing Norwegian, the factory ship was the final breakthrough that signalled disaster for the blue whale and many other species besides.

The first factory ship, *The Lancing*, was launched in 1925. It was designed to accompany a fleet of catcher boats and process the whales they caught. Unlike the floating factories these ships were entirely self-sufficient. They did not depend on land stations or harbours, but travelled in the open ocean for months on end. These seagoing abattoirs could hunt right up to the edge of the ice where the largest whales congregated to feed on krill. Enormous, squat, hulking vessels, the factory ships were fitted with a slipway in the stern up which the whale carcasses were hauled by a giant steel claw. They were astonishingly efficient; processing operations continued day and night on the spacious flensing decks and an entire adult blue whale could be disposed of in less than an hour. Factory ship whaling was not only much more efficient it was far less dangerous. While the whalers no longer risked life and limb for their occupation, the whales did not stand a chance. The slaughter escalated. In the 1930/31 season over 40,000 whales were killed in the Antarctic, three-quarters of which were blues.

Once killed and secured, whales were dragged up a slipway on to the factory ship.

Following the discovery of petroleum, whale oil was no longer used for lubrication and lighting but an entirely new market had emerged. At the beginning of the 20th century Europe's booming population faced a shortage of edible fats. Baleen whale oil was safe to eat but its unpleasant fishy smell and taste, and its tendency to go rancid, made it an unacceptable option. Then German industrial chemists solved the problem. They developed a technique of saturating the liquid oil with hydrogen, turning it into a solid and subduing its objectionable flavour. Hydrogenated whale oil could be used to make soap and margarine. At first consumers were not tempted by whale-oil products but by the 1930s, when chemists had perfected the process and made the oil truly palatable, they overcame their misgivings. Consequently more than 80% of the global take of whale oil was used in the manufacture of margarine – a cheap and popular substitute for butter. Conveniently a by-product of the chemical process was glycerine, used in the manufacture of dynamite.

Improved technology allowed the extraction of oil from the whale's meat and bones as well as the blubber. The rest of the carcass was processed with similar efficiency and in contrast to earlier enterprises very little went to waste. The remains of the meat and bones were boiled down to make a bonemeal for livestock feed and fertiliser. Vitamin A was extracted from the liver and the hormones insulin and corticotrophin were obtained from the glands and used to treat diabetes and arthritis, respectively. The tendons became tennis racket strings and surgical stitches, and the skin of toothed whales was cured as leather. The only part of the whale for which no use could be found was the baleen.

BY THE 1930s NORWAY was not reaping the Antarctic's riches alone. They had been joined by Britain, which became their main competitor early on. Later the Netherlands, USA, South Africa and the USSR all grabbed a slice of the action and as the threat of a Second World War loomed, Germany and Japan joined the hunt, stockpiling resources as they prepared to build empires. As the killing intensified the whaling nations became increasingly aware that the industry was out of control and needed reining in. The first international convention on whaling was introduced under the auspices of the League of Nations in 1935 and strengthened during subsequent negotiations in 1937. The new regulations prohibited the killing of right whales, calves and females with young, and set minimum size limits to prevent the slaughter of immature animals. The regulations also required the collation of catch statistics. Each factory ship was to carry an inspector but enforcement of the rules remained the responsibility of individual nations and there were no penalties for violations.

The measures were an unmitigated failure. The Japanese and Soviets refused to comply at all, while the nations that had agreed to observe the new regulations were hopelessly lax in their application. The 1937/38 season witnessed the most comprehensive slaughter to date. Some 55,000 whales died worldwide, over 45,000 of them in the Antarctic.

Further negotiations took place in 1938 but again they were defined by a lot of talk and no effective action. The whaling nations feigned a commitment towards a responsible strategy but even with their industry's future at stake they could not resist the allure of short-term profits and immediate returns on capital investment. Protection was extended to the Antarctic humpbacks, whose numbers had already dropped below the level of commercial viability, and a portion of the Southern Ocean was set aside as a sanctuary, although hardly any whaling took place there anyway.

In 1939 whalers were forced to cease whaling, not by the would-be regulators but by the Second World War. As conflict stormed across Europe, Antarctic whaling ground to a halt. Most of the factory ships were pressed into service as tankers and troop carriers and many were sunk. While the whaling nations turned their arms on each other the rorquals of the Southern Ocean enjoyed a brief respite.

Their peace was shattered almost as soon as the war ended. In 1946 the whaling nations came together to plan the future of the hunt. This time they avowed they would conserve their industry by sensible management of the world's whale stocks. After two weeks of negotiation the conference proudly announced the creation of the International Whaling Commission (IWC). From that time onwards the IWC has been at the heart of both whaling and whale conservation.

The IWC's remit was "to provide for the proper conservation of whale stocks and thus make possible the orderly development of the whaling industry". This was a commendable aim but from the very start the IWC found itself mired in a seemingly irreconcilable dispute between politicians, industrialists, scientists and, latterly, conservationists. The Commission incorporated a panel of science experts that would monitor whale populations, expand scientific knowledge of cetaceans and advise on their preservation. For the first time there was a limit on the number of whales that could be killed. Unfortunately, the quota size was determined using a system developed some years earlier. Known as the Blue Whale Unit (BWU), it was one of the most ill-conceived and destructive ideas in the history of the industry. A single BWU represented the average amount of whale product – namely 110 barrels of oil – that could be obtained from one blue whale. This imaginary unit was said to equal one blue whale, two fin whales, 2.5 humpbacks, or six sei whales. The BWU system made no allowance for the status of a particular species or stock. Since almost the same effort was required to catch, kill and process a blue whale as any of the others, the system made it all the more desirable a target. The Blue Whale Unit amounted to a warrant for the blue whale's extinction.

The IWC set the annual quota at 16,000 BWU. The whaling nations did not want to relinquish any potential takings and failed to agree on a formula for sharing it. The quota sparked frenetic competition as each nation tried to snatch as many whales as possible before the limit was reached. Instead of slowing the industry down, the quota drove investment in larger and faster catcher boats. By 1950 blue whales were becoming scarce. Between 325,000 and 360,000 had been killed since the concerted hunt for them started 25 years earlier. Laid end to end their carcasses would stretch all the way from the UK to South Africa. The whalers turned their focus to fin whales. Because they could take twice as many, numbers dropped rapidly. The whalers then targeted the sei whale.

Not only was the IWC using ineffective techniques to conserve whale stocks, it was also hamstrung by loopholes enshrined in its own constitution. The rules stated that any nation that did not wish to be bound by a decision could free itself simply by filing an objection. Since other members were unlikely to accept constraints rejected by a rival they would always follow suit. In practice every member had the power of veto and all decisions had to be unanimous. Even when regulations were passed they were not necessarily upheld, and the IWC had no authority to discipline violators. The organisation's impotence combined with the greed and lack of foresight of member nations was a recipe for disaster.

Throughout the 1950s, as biologists locked horns with politicians, the relationships between member nations spiralled into acrimony. In order to mollify its members and avoid its own dissolution, the IWC was forced to set limits that were known to be too high. In the latter part of the decade the quota was abandoned altogether, but within a few years it became clear that the whales and the hunt would not survive much longer and quotas were reintroduced. The blue whale finally received protection in 1965, but by then it was almost too late – in the previous season hunters had found only 20, all of which they killed.

By now whaling technology was state-of-the-art. Using radar, sonar, spotter planes and helicopters, the whalers were capable of winkling out the last few remaining whales, but they were unable to turn a profit. Eventually whaling nations had no choice but to close their operations. By 1968 the British, Dutch and Norwegians had retired their Antarctic fleets. They left the Southern Ocean to the Russians and Japanese who, finding few large whales to capture, turned their attention to the diminutive minke. The smallest of the rorquals, the minke had not until now been considered a worthwhile prey. They also resumed hunting of the sperm whale, principally in the North Pacific. From 1964 to 1974 more than a quarter of a million sperm whales were killed making up over half the global catch.

The BWU was finally abandoned in 1972. It was replaced with a system based on the principle of maximum sustainable yield. This aimed to divine the level at which exploitation would not reduce the breeding stock, on the assumption that the interest can be withdrawn without touching the capital. Although it seemed promising the new system was a fiasco. The scientists' knowledge of whale stocks and breeding patterns was insufficient and unrealistic quotas continued to be set. The IWC had comprehensively failed in its ambitions. It had overseen the destruction of the whaling industry and the near annihilation of the whales. And the situation was even worse than anyone realised.

IN 1993, AFTER THE COLD WAR had ended, former Soviet biologists revealed that the USSR had carried out extensive illegal whaling operations for decades. Since the late 1940s their factory fleets had wilfully ignored all regulations. They had slaughtered whales indiscriminately and published falsified data. They had killed young whales, protected species and females with calves, with ruinous consequences for whale conservation.

The discrepancy between reported and actual catches amounted to over 100,000 animals in the southern hemisphere alone. Half of these were notionally protected humpbacks: the Soviets had killed over 48,000 but had owned up to precisely 2710. They also took thousands of Antarctic blue whales after they had received full protection, which might explain why the population has not bounced back as expected. In the eastern North Pacific they slaughtered 372 of the few remaining right whales, striking a final blow from which the population has not recovered. The clues were there all along. In the late 1950s, as whale populations declined and arguments about quota sizes raged, the Soviets were busy building the largest factory ships the world had ever seen. They also vehemently opposed the introduction of international observer schemes.

The Soviets were not the only culprits. One of the worst offenders was Aristotle Onassis, the Greek shipping magnate. By adorning his vessels with the flags of Honduras and Panama, both countries outside the IWC, the ruthless tycoon was able to flout every single one of the Commission's rules. His factory ship, *Olympic Challenger*, cruised the Antarctic from 1951–1956 pillaging protected waters for whatever whales it encountered, be they endangered species or newborns. In a humiliating show of powerlessness the IWC could do nothing stop him. Onassis only ceased his slaughter when the Norwegians exerted intense pressure by publicising his activities.

Another notorious pirate ship was the *Sierra*. Liability for its crimes was carefully obscured in a tangle of red tape: flying the Somalian flag, it was jointly owned by Norwegian entrepreneurs and a Japanese fishing company, registered in Liechtenstein, crewed by South Africans and captained by a Norwegian. Its catch, labelled "product of Spain", was sold to Japan via the Ivory Coast. The *Sierra* patrolled the Atlantic throughout the

1970s until it was blown up by saboteurs in Lisbon harbour in 1980.

The saboteurs were eco-warriors, part of the fledgling environmental movement that had developed over the preceding decade and would bring the plight of the world's whales to the public's attention. The movement's first major player was Greenpeace. A rather motley collection of radicals, Greenpeace started campaigning against nuclear testing in 1969. In 1975 the organisation turned its attention to whaling. Greenpeace activists advocated non-violent protest. They became extremely sophisticated at using publicity-generating stunts and the media to spread their message and garner support.

Using small inflatable boats the fearless campaigners placed themselves between the harpoons of Soviet factory ships and the whales. Unimpressed, the Soviets simply fired their weapons over the protestors' heads. The activists were unable to stop the slaughter, but they filmed and photographed it, and broadcast haunting images of dead and dying whales and bloody effluent streaming from the ships' drains. The majority of the public had been unaware of the prevalence and brutality of whaling and the gruesome footage provoked an emotional response. The campaign built up momentum, attracting supporters from all walks of life. Once perceived as a natural resource with no more intrinsic value than timber or coal, the whale suddenly became a totemic symbol – the poster animal for all those committed to saving the planet.

The IWC was under pressure. Some of its members started lobbying for a moratorium on all commercial whaling. Influenced by the environmentalists, they argued that this was the only foolproof method to safeguard the whales. In 1982 a groundswell of support led to the necessary three-quarters majority being obtained and the moratorium was fully in place by 1986.

OVER THE EIGHT DECADES following the opening of the Antarctic grounds in 1904 the whaling industry was responsible for the deaths of over two million whales in the southern hemisphere. Some species are recovering. Humpbacks, like gray whales, have proved very resilient and are showing strong growth rates around the world although they still number less than 20% of the pre-whaling stock. Others have not fared so well. Antarctic blue whales and fin whales were reduced to between 1% and 10% of their original numbers and they remain highly endangered. Little is known of their smaller cousin, the sei whale, but they are rarely encountered.

Technology gave the modern whalers power and reach far beyond that of their ill-equipped predecessors, but by deploying it indiscriminately they only hastened their own downfall. Considerable effort is now being made to save those species that the whaling industry almost eradicated, but in many cases success has not been achieved. Additionally, the 1986 moratorium did not precipitate the end of all whaling – whales, as well as dolphins and porpoises, are still killed in their thousands every year and the pressure to resume commercial whaling is mounting.

A conflict of interests

On modern whaling

Tokyo's Tsukiji fish market is the largest of its kind in the world. Situated in what could pass for an aircraft hangar, it boasts thousands of stalls selling a mind-boggling variety of seafood. There are rows of shimmering tuna, mounds of rubbery octopus tentacles, tanks of lobsters and crayfish exploring their confines with quivering feelers, and buckets of live eels. Tucked away towards the back and easily overlooked there is also a single stall specialising entirely in whale products. It sells slabs of claret-coloured whale meat, diced blubber and 'whale bacon' wrapped in plastic. These products are destined for Japan's few remaining whale restaurants where diners feast on such delicacies as whale heart and tongue, whale stew and whale sushi.

The stall is an innocuous presence, a quiet corner amid the hustle and bustle of the market, but it is testament to an ongoing and increasingly bitter international dispute. The questions firing this disagreement seem simple enough: should whales and dolphins

Whale meat on sale at Tokyo's Tsukiji fish market.

ever be killed and traded for profit? Can whale hunting ever be truly sustainable or do we run the risk of history repeating itself?

Within the IWC, whose membership has swelled from the original 14 members to more than 60, there are two clearly defined and diametrically opposed camps: those who are for and those who are against whaling. Over time the positions of the pro- and anti-whaling blocs have grown increasingly polarised. The organisation has become riven by politics and stymied by its own rules. During emotionally charged and often hostile annual meetings both sides accuse their opponents of hypocrisy, obduracy, and of twisting the facts to suit their needs. For the rest of the year both sides make significant political and financial investment to secure the support of lawmakers, other IWC members and the general public.

Although the majority of whaling nations responded to the IWC's 1986 ruling by disbanding their whaling fleets, a minority reacted with defiance and continued to whale under a variety of different guises. Since the moratorium was enacted over 25,000 great whales have been deliberately killed. The countries at the forefront of whaling today are Japan and Norway. Both nations whale in ways that are legal but highly controversial. Japan conducts 'scientific whaling' by invoking an exemption in the convention that established the IWC, the International Convention for the Regulation of Whaling (ICRW). The exemption allows countries to take whales for the purposes of scientific research. Norway, another whale-eating nation, takes advantage of a different loophole: any signatory can sidestep a particular rule by lodging a formal objection to it. In 1992 Norway objected to the moratorium and returned to whaling.

Despite widespread international condemnation and repeated calls from the IWC to cease their whaling activities, both nations have steadily increased the number of whales they catch. Norway, which pursues minke whales in the northeast Atlantic, caught between 200 and 600 animals per year throughout the 1990s. In 2005 it awarded itself an enlarged quota of 796 whales, of which 639 were caught, and announced plans to further raise this allowance from 2006. Japan conducts two separate scientific whaling operations: JARPA and JARPN. The JARPA programme takes place in Antarctica within the boundaries of the Southern Ocean Sanctuary, a supposedly safe haven for all great whales established by the IWC in 1994. Having self-allocated an annual quota of 440 minke whales for some time, it was re-launched as the more ambitious JARPA II in 2005. Of an intended haul of 935 minke whales, 853 were harvested along with ten fin whales. The fin whale was decimated during the heyday of Antarctic whaling and is still endangered, so the decision to resume its slaughter appalled other nations. The controversy does not stop there – Japan provoked worldwide anger when it announced its intention to take 50 fin whales and 50 humpback whales per year starting in 2007. The JARPN programme, which operates in the North Pacific, self-awards an annual take of 220 minke whales, 100 sei whales, 50 Bryde's whales and ten sperm whales.

Iceland also conducts a scientific whaling programme, but on a much smaller scale. Having left the IWC in 1992 it rejoined in 2001 and two years later submitted a proposal to take 500 whales over two years, including fin whales, sei whales and minke whales. It was forced to scale back its plans by tremendous international opposition and since 2003 has taken up to 39 minke whales a year.

Since the whaling debate was first ignited, primarily by the Greenpeace protests in the 1970s, it has become extremely complex. The issue now incorporates an intricate web of often conflicting ideas, beliefs and scientific evidence. The anti-whaling crusaders, led by the UK, Australia and New Zealand – some of the foremost whaling nations of old – argue that whaling is unsustainable, cruel, impossible to control and unnecessary. In these countries scientists tend to take a pro-conservation stance and public opinion concurs; whales are perceived as intelligent, sentient, beautiful animals that merit special protection.

The whalers are infuriated by what they see as an arbitrary veto on their right to exploit natural resources. They argue that the anti-whaling advocates are slaves to sentiment, preaching an unacceptable form of cultural and culinary imperialism. In their opinion conservationists exaggerate the intelligence of whales and their affinity to humans in order to convince the public that their killing is tantamount to homicide. The Norwegian anthropologist Arne Kalland has coined the term 'super whale' to describe a purely mythical beast which has been created and marketed by environmentalists. It is the world's largest animal with the largest brain, it is friendly, sings, loves its children, is morally good and is threatened. Some of these characteristics are true for some whales, but no species exhibits them all. The more cynical pro-whalers believe that their adversaries are merely armchair environmentalists 'eco-posturing' about the plight of whales in other parts of the world while remaining blind to the intensive farming practices and destruction of wild habitats that take place in their own countries.

Every year the pro-whaling faction argues that while some whale populations remain endangered, others could support a carefully controlled whaling regime. And every year their opponents draw on a raft of other arguments to block them. So far the anti-whaling lobby has prevailed but their long-held majority is gradually being eroded. At the IWC's 2006 meeting, held on the Caribbean island of St Kitts, the pro-whaling nations lost four key votes but won one. A resolution proposed by Japan to declare that the moratorium on commercial whaling was "no longer necessary" was passed by 33 votes to 32. The victory was purely symbolic as a simple majority is insufficient to overturn the moratorium – for that a 75% majority is required – but conservationists fear that this shift in power could mark a turning point. They are gravely concerned that the Commission's agenda will focus increasingly on hunting rather than conservation and that a return to commercial whaling is imminent.

THE QUESTION OF NUMBERS – how many whales there are in the sea, how many there were before commercial whaling began, and at what level their populations could support renewed commercial whaling – is central to the debate. But the science of estimating whale numbers is notoriously difficult. Because the animals are highly mobile, usually spread over large areas, and spend considerable time out of sight beneath the water's surface, gathering precise information about population sizes is impossible. Scientists conduct surveys from large, oceanographic research vessels and aircraft: numbers of cetaceans spotted over a defined area, or along imaginary parallel transect lines, are extrapolated via complex mathematical formulae to give the best possible estimation of abundance.

In 1993, following many of years of discussion about the management of whaling, the IWC adopted a proposed regulatory system. The Revised Management Scheme (RMS) incorporates guidelines on catch limits, inspection and observation programmes, compliance and animal welfare considerations. Central to the scheme is the Revised Management Procedure (RMP), a method for calculating sustainable quotas. The RMP is designed to provide complete protection for stocks that fall below 54% of the levels that existed before the start of commercial whaling. Its safe application is therefore contingent on the availability of trustworthy information about the sizes of whale stocks, and for this reason many anti-whalers question its efficacy. Not only is the science of whale-counting inexact, but abundance estimates are often supplied by whaling interests who may be influenced by their broader agenda. Estimates of historical whale populations often depend on old catch records which, although detailed, were not compiled according to scientific principles.

The minke whale, the animal that sustains most of the whaling that takes place today, is at the heart of debate. With a range that extends from the poles to the tropics, the minke is the smallest member of the rorqual family. Females grow to around

10.8 m (35 ft) in the Antarctic and 9.2 m (30 ft) in the northern hemisphere, while males measure a metre or two less. The whale's curious name comes from Norway. One story has it that a whale spotter named Meincke, on the look out for blue whales, incorrectly sounded the alarm on sighting a minke. To his chagrin the smallest rorqual then became popularly known as Minke's whale. The minke has a slender, streamlined body, a distinctive triangular-shaped head, and a narrow pointed snout. Its body is dark grey to black on the back, paling to white on the belly and undersides of the flippers. The northern hemisphere whales sport an eye-catching diagonal white band on the upper surface of each flipper. The minke's twin blow is relatively inconspicuous, so whalers usually require calm waters to hunt them.

The world's major minke whale populations are found in the North Atlantic, where they are hunted by the Norwegians, and in

Minke whales fleeing a Japanese ship in Antarctica during the 2005/06 scientific whaling season.

the North Pacific and Southern Ocean, where they are hunted by the Japanese. Japan consistently claims that around 760,000 minke whales frolic in Antarctic waters, and that since this represents a comfortable 90% of the pre-exploitation population, the minke is ripe for harvesting. But this figure was produced by the Institute of Cetacean Research (ICR), Japan's main whaling body, and many experts dispute it. In 2001 the IWC's Scientific Committee – an advisory panel of around 120 cetacean specialists – considered more recent data and warned that today's Antarctic minke population may number less than half that amount.

Assumptions about historical population sizes are also being questioned. Researchers in the USA have delved into the last million years of minke whale history by deciphering information locked in the whales' genes. The level of genetic variation in animals alive today indicates that the Antarctic may once have been home to an astonishing 1.5 million minke whales. If this figure is accurate, the RMP's 54% protection level would grant the whales immunity from exploitation even if Japan's claim about today's robust population were correct.

The RMP's detractors argue that the model makes fundamental and potentially disastrous assumptions about whale population dynamics. Quotas would be established according to geography, but without the fine-tuning necessary to account for the exact composition of local whale stocks. In the case of the minke whale, the RMP does not allow for the likely existence of two distinct species in the Southern Ocean. Genetic research carried out during the 1990s revealed that Antarctica is probably home to both the Antarctic minke whale, found only in waters south of the equator, and the dwarf minke whale, a small form of the common minke which is also found in the northern hemisphere.

ABUNDANCE DEBATES ASIDE, many conservationists believe that commercial whalers simply cannot be trusted to play by the rules. They are concerned that if whale meat is legally procured and traded, it will mask an uncontrolled black market in whale products. The annals of whaling are filled with tales of duplicity. In the period after the Second World War, Japanese commercial whaling was monitored by national inspectors who were routinely duped into under-reporting catch statistics. The whaling companies distracted the inspectors with expensive meals and excursions, and pooled information on the officials' whereabouts so that whalers could safely land illegal catches when the coast was clear. And as Soviet whalers demonstrated in the 1960s and 1970s, even large-scale piracy is impossible to police on the high seas.

More recently, Japan has failed to prevent illegally caught whale meat being traded under cover of its scientific whaling programme. In the 1990s investigators testing whale products on sale in Japanese shops, markets and restaurants found the meat of notionally protected fin, humpback and blue whales, as well as several species of dolphin and porpoise mislabelled as whale. Additionally, the first six tonnes of a 60 tonne consignment of whale meat, disguised as a mackerel shipment, were discovered being smuggled from Norway to Japan in 1996. And in the summer of 1997, sailors on transatlantic yachts near the Azores reported seeing dead and dying whales floating on the surface and tied to marker buoys.

A solution has been proposed in the form of an international database that would hold the DNA of each animal caught. Whale products could be randomly sampled from the market place and checked against the database to verify their source. But the idea is floundering because stakeholders cannot reach agreement on its administration. Some believe that it should be managed centrally by the IWC, which would also be responsible for the inspection of whaling activities, while whaling nations would prefer to be in charge of their own operations. Understandably, the fears of conservation groups will not be assuaged if independence is not adopted as a guiding paradigm.

WITH THE MORATORIUM STILL in place, the RMS remains a purely theoretical system of management. Meanwhile, the world's most prodigious whaling nation is Japan. According to the rules of the ICRW, the by-products of scientific research can, and in fact should, be sold commercially. The sale of whale meat and blubber largely funds Japan's research programmes, which are organised by the Institute of Cetacean Research (ICR).

A key objective of both Japan's Antarctic and Pacific enterprises is the gathering of detailed information about the local minke whale populations. Researchers on JARPN, the Pacific programme, are also investigating whether or not the whales are responsible for the precipitous decline observed in commercial fish stocks. That whales should be culled to protect fish resources is a common refrain of pro-whaling nations.

So is there any truth in the claim? In 2000, JARPN researchers found that Bryde's whales prefer Japanese anchovies, and that 90% of the stomach contents of minke whales comprised a blend of anchovies and two other commercially fished species – walleye pollock and Pacific saury. Minke whales have also been found to eat significant quantities of cod, herring and capelin in the Greater Barents Sea, and cod in Icelandic waters. Taking the JARPN observations as their cue, the ICR estimated that whales devour between 250 and 500 million tonnes of fish a year – three to six times the amount scooped from the oceans by the world's fishing fleets. They then adopted the upper estimate as fact and issued press releases and leaflets warning that voracious cetaceans were compromising global food security.

Research conducted by cetacean experts elsewhere generally draws very different conclusions. A number of studies have shown that the feeding grounds of whales and commercial fishing grounds rarely overlap, with most large cetaceans consuming the majority of their intake in remote polar regions. When the great whales appear elsewhere, they are usually migrating or breeding – periods when they feed very little. Baleen whales eat mainly krill, although they also consume some small fish species, while the sperm whale preys primarily upon squid, including many deep water species that are not fished commercially. Ultimately there may be an element of truth in claims of competition in specific areas. Crucially, however, whales and humans are not competing for fish at a global level.

But even if whales were competing with humans for certain fish, would their slaughter be justified and would it solve the problem? Marine ecosystems and food webs are extremely complex and often poorly understood. Multiple factors affect the health of fish stocks and simple cause-and-effect relationships rarely exist, so it is impossible to predict what impact the removal of one species will have on another. Furthermore, the animals that eat the most fish are not cetaceans, but other fish.

Conservationists point to the fact that historically the oceans teemed with both whales and fish. It is only since humans started fishing on an industrial scale that fish populations have crashed. They argue, convincingly, that whale populations, being much smaller now than they were in the past, cannot be the cause of the problem. Instead they are merely convenient scapegoats. The belief that fish yields will be improved by eliminating whales, rather than switching to a sustainable fishing regime is, they say, naive at best.

A similarly contentious suggestion is that growing minke whale populations represent the unnatural bloom of a weed-like species, thriving now that its competitors have been removed. Some Japanese scientists believe that the rampant proliferation of minke whales could be stunting the recovery of other species such as blue and fin whales – yet another reason to cull them. But this hypothesis has been dismissed as a fallacy by a number of scien-

Japanese scientific whalers defend their actions.

tists from other countries whose case is boosted by genetic research indicating that the minke whale may have once numbered 1.5 million in the Antarctic alone.

The IWC has repeatedly asked Japan to abandon its current scientific whaling programmes. Much of the research could be done with the use of benign methods such as DNA studies and biopsy sampling. But Japan insists its lethal takes are necessary. Conservation groups believe the reason for this is that the scientific whalers have an ulterior motive. They reckon that the research programmes are a pretence that serve to keep the industry alive: without them the fleet would be disbanded, crew members would find other jobs, and a return to commercial whaling would move out of reach in a practical sense. Should the moratorium be lifted, the financial cost of resuscitating a defunct industry would be prohibitive. In 1985 the Japanese Minister for Fisheries, Moriyoshi Sato, admitted as much when he observed that, in response to the IWC's moratorium, "the government [of Japan] will do its utmost to find ways to maintain the nation's whaling in the form of research or other forms."

THE WHALING DEBATE covers a much broader spectrum of topics than just stock numbers and dietary preferences. There is also the question of ethics. Central to this issue is the contention that if a humane death cannot be guaranteed, then whales should not be hunted at all. Despite significant technological advances, there is still no sure-fire way to swiftly kill a swimming animal from a moving ship.

Norway and Japan have greatly improved the efficiency of their hunting techniques. Following its prohibition by the IWC, they have for the most part relinquished the 'cold' (non-explosive) harpoon in favour of the explosive penthrite grenade. This is designed to penetrate about 30 cm (12 in) into the whale's body near the base of the skull and detonate, shattering the spinal cord and mashing the brain with lethal shockwaves. If the initial strike fails to kill, whalers finish the job using a second harpoon or rifle. Despite the ban on cold harpoons, Japan still uses them as a secondary killing method in its North Pacific operation.

Although the average time to death is a relatively speedy two minutes, some animals take considerably longer; in 1993 a minke whale harpooned by the Norwegians lingered for nearly an hour. The track records of the two main whaling nations differ markedly: in the 2002 season 80.7% of the whales killed by the Norwegians died more or less instantaneously, but only 40.2% of those killed by the Japanese suffered so briefly. The two countries use the same techniques, but while the Norwegians aim at or just behind the whale's head to achieve the quickest possible kill, the Japanese hunters sometimes deliberately aim elsewhere. They do this to avoid damaging the animal's ear plugs, because they use them to estimate the whale's age.

Anti-whalers argue that similar treatment of a land mammal would not be tolerated. Strict rules govern the killing of farm animals in abattoirs – they must be stunned first and then dispatched while unconscious. Anti-whalers are also concerned that the methods used are not adapted to the precise requirements of each target species; the techniques developed to kill the relatively diminutive minke, for example, may not be as effective when used on the larger sperm and fin whales. They further question the credibility of 'time to death' statistics produced by whaling nations. According to current IWC guidelines, whales are dead if the lower jaw and flippers have become limp, or the animal sinks without movement. But animal welfare experts have suggested that these diagnostic benchmarks may not be adequate. They believe that the special physiological and anatomical adaptations of an air-breathing, deep-sea diving mammal may make it difficult to determine whether an individual is alive or dead. Whales hold unusually plentiful stocks of oxygen in their tissues, which may sustain life even when the animal appears to have breathed its last.

This outpouring of concern bemuses the whalers. They consider it preposterous that whales are held in such respect when other farm and game animals are exploited without qualm. They contend that whales should not be accorded a higher status than the other wild animals, such as elk, deer and kangaroos, that are killed in their thousands every year, and accuse their adversaries of operating double standards. The anti-whalers counter that unlike deer and other game animals, whales have not evolved as prey species. They are not physiologically equipped for the chase and are likely to endure greater pathological stress. This may be true, but whales enjoy a long and liberated life in the sea before a relatively short period of suffering leads to death – whether they have a better overall experience than a battery chicken, or intensively-reared pig, is a matter for conjecture.

Ultimately, the pain and stress-free killing of a whale in the wild can never be guaranteed. Technicalities and statistics aside, the anti-whalers cannot accept the subjection of a whale to this inevitable and unnecessary suffering. For the whalers, the end justifies the means, and their rights and desires reasonably prevail over these animals, as over so many others.

THE WHALING DEBATE has become intensely political. Both the pro- and anti-whalers are waging a very public battle to win over hearts and minds. Of all the whaling nations, Japan has mounted the most determined campaign. Supported by nationalist politicians, its whaling lobby buys advertising space in newspapers and magazines and distributes glossy pamphlets to promote its cause. It vindicates its fervour by claiming that the hunting and eating of whales is a traditional and vital part of Japanese culture. This is highly contentious. Although whales have been hunted offshore by a smattering of coastal communities for centuries, it was only in the years preceding the Second World War that the nation embarked on deep-sea whaling in distant oceans and consumption of whale meat spread inland. After the war, General MacArthur, who led the USA's occupation of Japan, spearheaded the expansion of the industry in order to boost the protein intake of a malnourished population. Cheap and readily available, whale meat came to account for 30% of all meat consumption and until the 1970s was routinely served to children for school lunches. Then as whale populations dwindled, production dropped and consumption declined.

Whether or not the majority of Japanese actually want to eat whale meat, as their political representatives insist, is another moot point. A survey conducted by the *Asahi Shimbun* newspaper in 2002 found that only 4% of 3000 respondents ate it regularly, while 53% had not eaten it since school and 33% had never tasted it at all. The whaling industry is trying to overcome this obstacle by developing innovative products such as whale burgers and blubber ice cream, designed to appeal to the younger generation. It also subsidises whale meat sales in school lunches.

At present, though, it seems likely that at least some of the extra produce generated by the enhanced quotas will end up in cold storage.

In order to fulfil its whaling ambitions, Japan needs to win further victories at the IWC. A simple majority of 51% on key votes would enable them and the other pro-whaling nations to abolish the Commission's work on conservation and animal welfare, promote trade in whale products, and make the presently open ballots secret – measures which would bring their ultimate goal closer.

To this end Japan has been accused of buying the votes of other, poorer IWC members. According to their critics Japanese whaling interests have brazenly courted politicians and senior officials from a number of Pacific, Caribbean and African nations, showering them with generous aid packages and other sweeteners such as lavish, all-expense-paid trips to Japan. The Japanese dismiss these allegations as nonsense, but their schemes were exposed in 2000 when the Minister for the Environment and Fisheries of Dominica unexpectedly resigned. This tiny island state promotes itself as a holiday retreat for nature lovers and as the Caribbean's premier whale-watching destination. The minister claimed that he had been pressured by his government to vote in favour of whaling at the next IWC meeting, and had felt unacceptably compromised. Despite initial denials of behind-the-scenes coercion, a government official later admitted that Japan had furnished Dominica with a new fish processing plant and a fleet of Japanese cars, and had also paid their annual IWC membership fee.

But the Japanese are not alone in recruiting new allies for such purposes. Their tactics mirror those used by the conservation lobby to marshal support for the vote in favour of the moratorium in the 1980s. Consequently, both sides in the debate count various landlocked nations with no historical interest in whaling whatsoever among their numbers, including Mongolia (pro-whaling) and the Czech Republic (anti-whaling). Japan's complaint is that the conservationists' allies are simply boosting their green credentials by signing up to 'save the whale', and frustrating the whaling lobby without a real appreciation of the issues at stake.

Norway is similarly vexed by the intransigence of the IWC's anti-whaling bloc. It has been a driving force in the establishment of various organisations that hope to challenge the IWC's global supremacy on the regulation of whaling. In 1992 the fisheries ministries of Norway and Iceland and the home rule governments of the Faroe Islands and Greenland set up the North Atlantic Marine Mammals Commission (NAMMCO) in response to the IWC's moratorium on commercial whaling. Controversial from the outset, NAMMCO has no authority under international law to act as either an international or regional regulatory body, and its bid to supersede the IWC in the North Atlantic has so far been unsuccessful. The High North Alliance, another organisation with a similar agenda, was founded in Norway in 1990 to protect "the rights of whalers, sealers and fishermen to harvest renewable resources in accordance with the principle of sustainable management".

Of all the organisations that do not recognise the legal competence of these challengers, the Convention on the International Trade in Endangered Species (CITES) is perhaps the most important. Since 1979 CITES has officially recognised the IWC as the lead organisation responsible for managing whales and whaling. In cooperation with the IWC's moratorium, it exercises a complete ban on the international commercial trade in whale meat. Japan and Norway have strived to have the trade ban lifted ever since its instigation, and contest the assumption that CITES automatically takes its lead from the IWC.

THE IWC's MORATORIUM is not a blanket ban on all whaling activities. Some native peoples have been granted exemption to carry out 'aboriginal subsistence whaling' with special quotas granted according to advice given by the Scientific Committee. Greenlanders receive the largest quota: they are currently entitled to take 187 minke whales and ten fin whales each year. The Chukotka people, who inhabit a remote part of eastern Siberia, are permitted to take up to 140 gray whales from the northeast Pacific population annually, while the handful of people who maintain the tiny industry on the island of Bequia, part of the St Vincent and the Grenadines island group, take four humpback whales a year.

In the USA, the Inupiat and Yup'ik people of Alaska are authorised to take up to 67 bowhead whales a year from the 10,000-strong Bering-Chukchi-Beaufort Seas population. Although the hunt has attracted criticism from some conservation groups, the Eskimo whalers make a compelling case for their right to practice long-held cultural traditions of killing and eating whales. Another controversial bowhead hunt is operated in the eastern Arctic by Canadian Inuit. Canada left the IWC in 1982 and has allowed aboriginal hunting to proliferate. Anti-whalers have accused the Canadian government of forsaking its conservation responsibilities for the sake of political expediency. However, the bowhead stock in question numbers around 8000 and is steadily growing. The Inuit are permitted to take, on average, one whale each year so their impact is minimal.

Knowledge of bowhead whale population dynamics is limited but recent studies carried out in the USA have disclosed some surprising information. Researchers have discovered that bowhead

An indigenous hunter in Greenland tows home his catch, a beluga whale.

whales, not giant tortoises, may be the longest-lived animals in the world. Stone and ivory harpoon heads dating from the 18th century have been found embedded in the blubber of bowheads caught in Alaska. Further evidence of the whales' longevity has been brought to light by research on their eye lenses. The lenses, which are adapted to allow underwater focusing, are spherical structures consisting of numerous protein sheets layered like an onion. Chemical changes in aspartic acid, one of the amino acids in the protein, can be quantified to determine the age of the animal. Of the whales studied, four were found to be over 100 years old, while one had achieved a staggering 211 years. Longer-lived animals tend to reproduce and replenish stocks at a slow rate, making them especially vulnerable to exploitation. The bow-heads targeted by North American Inuit are prospering, but these revelations highlight the need for reliable information on cetacean population dynamics before critical decisions about hunting quotas are taken.

Although the numbers of whales killed under the banner of aboriginal subsistence hunting are usually quite small, the socio-political implications can be far-reaching. In recent years some indigenous groups have been courted by commercial whaling interests in an attempt to build pro-whaling alliances, broaden the debate and blur the boundaries that define aboriginal and commercial operations. The distinction is genuinely nebulous since the commonly used terms 'aboriginal' and 'subsistence' are not officially defined by the ICRW. Japan and Norway often contend that their coastal communities were founded on whaling and should be afforded aboriginal status even though they conduct commercial trade. In theory the products of aboriginal subsistence hunting should all be consumed locally and not sold for profit, but in practice this is not always the case: some of the meat generated by the Greenlandic hunt can be found on sale in local supermarkets.

The modernisation of aboriginal hunts, and the significance of technological progress for the welfare of whales killed, pro-vides fertile ground for debate. Traditional hunting methods are often less efficient than modern ones – whales take longer to die and greater numbers are struck and lost. Many aboriginal groups now hunt equipped with a modern armoury, but this has pro-voked the ire of some anti-whaling groups who feel that the hunt must remain traditional if its protagonists justify its existence by claiming its cultural value. However, old-fashioned methods are typically less humane and by their own admission the limitation of the animals' suffering should be paramount.

Central to the pro-whalers' argument is that in prioritising the rights of animals the conservationists are instead driving time-honoured whaling cultures to extinction. Some conservationists might agree, because they believe that the traditions of societies that do not need to eat whale meat to survive should be re-evaluated. For them, the killing of whales should go the way of other once-popular pastimes such as bear-baiting and throwing Christians to the lions.

The most reasoned commentators allow that aboriginal cultures can adopt modern technology to keep pace with a changing world while retaining the fundaments of their historical customs. For many communities the hunting of whales, the rituals of meat distribution, and the preparation and taste of the food are irreplaceable cultural observances. In the face of global cultural homogenisation, distinctive cultures should be safeguarded rather than suppressed. But the whales on which those cultures depend warrant protection, too. We must strike a balance between the needs of native peoples and the importance of conserving whales. This can only be achieved with open dialogue, transparency, ongoing evaluation of the health of whale populations, and active negotiation as to what does and does not constitute aboriginal whaling.

WHALERS DO NOT TARGET only the larger cetaceans. Many thousands of smaller whales, dolphins and porpoises are killed, legally, around the world every year. These small cetaceans are not protected by the IWC because their names are not listed in its Annex of Nomenclature. Drawn up in 1946, this inventory covers only the species relevant to whaling concerns at the time – all the baleen whales except the pygmy right whale, plus the sperm whale, an odontocete. In theory these are the 'great whales' measuring more than 9 m (30 ft) in length, but in reality some whales excluded from the list, such as Baird's beaked whale, are larger than the minke whale which is included. Undoubtedly an anomaly of history, the scope of the IWC's jurisdiction is a long-standing cause of dispute.

Some IWC members wish to expand the Commission's remit to cover all cetaceans. They are concerned that large-scale slaughter, which is neither monitored nor controlled, could have a serious impact on cetacean populations. This adjustment would indeed make better sense and bring the ICRW in line with other international treaties. But the states that hunt small cetaceans tend to do so within their own coastal waters. They argue that a change to the IWC's rules would intrude upon their sovereign right to control national resources.

The conservationists have had some successes. Until the mid 1990s as many as 20,000 small cetaceans, chiefly dusky dolphins and Burmeister's porpoises, were hunted along the coast of Peru. The industry proved extremely lucrative for the hunters but was on course to wipe out the animals on which it was based. International campaigns were mounted and eventually government legislation brought the killing to an end.

In other parts of the world, however, small cetaceans are still routinely killed for their meat, as scapegoats for badly managed fisheries, and for use as crab bait, fertiliser and chicken meal. Aboriginal whalers take around 2000 beluga whales, 1000 narwhals and numerous dolphins and porpoises in the Arctic regions of Canada, the USA, Greenland and Russia. They use the oil for lighting and cooking, and eat the meat, blubber and skin. Small cetaceans are also slaughtered commercially. Throughout the Caribbean around 400 pilot whales are killed annually, along with common dolphins, spinner dolphins, Atlantic spotted dolphins, bottlenose dolphins, melon-headed whales, false killer whales and pygmy killer whales. But the nation responsible for the greatest killing of small cetaceans is Japan, which slaughters 17,000 to 20,000 small whales, dolphins and porpoises every year. Japanese hunters pursue 16 of the 21 species of small cetacean that live in their coastal waters, but their primary target is Dall's porpoise. The industry this stocky, black-and-white creature supports constitutes the largest direct kill of cetaceans in the world. Until 1987 the annual take hovered around the 10,000 mark, but in 1988 it soared to 40,000. Under pressure from the IWC, which exerts some power despite having no formal authority, the govern-

Sun-dried whale meat in St Vincent and the Grenadines.

ment of Japan scaled back the hunt to around 17,000 animals a year. The hunt yields hundreds of tonnes of meat that are sold throughout the country.

Although the Japanese enterprise is the most prolific of the small cetacean hunts, perhaps the most notorious takes place in the Faroe Islands, an archipelago of 18 islands shaped like an arrowhead in the North Atlantic roughly midway between Norway and Iceland. The Faroese are descended from Vikings who settled there in the ninth century. For hundreds of years they have been operating the *grind*, a drive-hunt that is both celebrated and reviled. The principal target of the *grind* is the long-finned pilot whale, but northern bottlenose whales and Atlantic white-sided dolphins are occasionally caught, too. Rules guiding the distribution of whale meat were established as early as 1298, and tax accounts date back to 1584. In the 19th century the early regulations were formally worked up into the 'Grind Law', which still governs the hunt today.

Early whalers called the long-finned pilot whales 'potheads' because they thought their heads resembled black iron cooking pots. Females can reach 6 m (20 ft) in length, while males grow to around 8 m (26 ft). They are family animals that travel in pods of between ten and 50 individuals, although groupings of 100 are not uncommon. They feed primarily on squid and their seasonal movements follow the migration routes of their prey.

As with many of the odontocetes, females form the stable nucleus of the family pods, although many males remain with their natal groups for life. Immensely strong social bonds keep the group united and the long-finned pilot whale is thought to be subject to more mass strandings than any other cetacean. So unshakeable is the instinct to stick together that during rescue efforts individuals that have been refloated may hurl themselves back onto the shore if other members are still alive there. The whalers exploit these social ties when they drive the whales.

During the *grind*, the hunters steer their boats into a semi-circle behind the pod, blocking the whales' escape route out to sea. The whales are then goaded towards the shore. Once one member of the pod beaches itself, the rest quickly follow suit. The hunters wade out into the water to haul in any animals that remain floating onto the shore using a steel instrument called a *gaff*, and then kill the whales with a special knife called a *grindaknívur*. This is driven into the neck, behind the blowhole. Ideally, the knife severs the spinal cord and surrounding arteries, causing a swift drop in blood pressure in the brain.

The tradition may be ancient but the technology used today is not. While the first sighting of whales was once communicated across the islands with burning fires and large sheets spread over the hillsides, radios and telephones now allow a much speedier response. Once shepherded by rowers, the whales are now driven from motorised boats. These are not only faster but can travel further out to sea to coax outlying animals into shore. As the hunt has become more efficient, so kill rates have risen. During the 1980s over 20,000 long-finned pilot whales were slaughtered in the Faroe Islands, more than ever before in the *grind's* long history. The annual take has subsequently stabilised at around 1000 whales a year.

The hunt has been the target of international campaigns by environmental groups since the mid 1980s. Campaigners are concerned that it may permanently damage whale stocks; a 1989 survey indicated that the population may number a healthy 778,000 but conservationists consider this figure to be unreliable. The hunt is unselective, with young whales and pregnant and lactating females taken along with the rest. The Faroese are also accused of cruelty. In the past the steel *gaffs* used to heave the whales onto the shore were sharp hooks that snagged in the animal's blubber. In recent years whalers have replaced these *gaffs*

Long-finned pilot whales caught during the *grind*.

with blunt instruments that they insert into the whales' blow-holes, in a bid to improve welfare. Anti-whaling groups are not convinced however; they have expressed concern that blocking the airway and irritating its sensitive nerve-rich lining may cause panic and pain.

The Faroese whalers claim that the *grind* is central to their unique national identity. Their culture is permeated by machismo and influenced by deep-rooted traditions of men battling against the elements to feed their families. But the Faroe Islands have a relatively affluent economy built on fishing and its people no longer need to wage war with nature to survive. Times have changed, and many believe that the Faroese should procure their food in the same ways as the rest of the developed world.

For now the hunt continues, but it is coming under threat from another, unexpected source. According to the Grind Law, the spoils from the hunt should be distributed evenly among local people, whether they participated in the *grind* or not. But not everyone can eat their share. In the early 1990s pilot whale meat and blubber were found to contain a medley of toxic contaminants that pose a serious health risk. The Faroese Health Authority responded by issuing advice recommending that meat and blubber should not be eaten more than once or twice a month; that pregnant and nursing women, and those planning to conceive, should steer clear of it altogether; and that the liver and kidneys, as repositories of toxins, should not be eaten by anyone. These restrictions are somewhat at odds with the insistence that the pilot whale is an important staple of the Faroese diet. Despite the current struggle to maintain the hunt, the perils of eating its fruits may ultimately lead to its cessation.

Japanese and Norwegian consumers are also at risk. Their governments chose to ignore this when they started advertising the health benefits of eating whale meat in the early 1990s. They

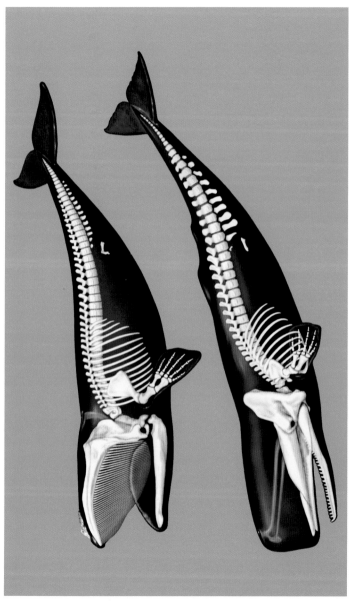

Anatomy of the right whale (top). Anatomy of the sperm whale (bottom).

Male narwhals are endowed with a 3 m (10 ft) long tusk (top). The Arctic-dwelling bowhead whale can ram its way through ice 50 cm (20 in) thick (bottom).

Inside the sperm whale's cavernous head is the largest brain of any living being.

The humpback whale is famed for its spectacular breaching behaviour.

The largest animal that has ever lived, the blue whale can grow to over 30 m (100 ft) in length (top). Hunters kill more Dall's porpoises than any other cetacean (bottom).

Short-beaked common dolphins in the Gulf of California.

The delightful but beleaguered beluga whale.

With their blunt heads and grey skin scored with white scratches, Risso's dolphins are easy to identify.

pointed to the startlingly low incidence of coronary heart disease and cardiovascular complaints among Inuit populations whose diet consists largely of fish and marine mammals. But although cetacean meat was once extremely nutritious, the consumption of many species is now a hazardous activity. In Japan the meat of smaller, inshore species such as Dall's porpoise – which frequently carry dangerously high toxic burdens – is often fraudulently labelled and sold as whale meat, leaving the consumer both mis-informed and exposed.

THE ICRW IS OUT OF STEP with the modern world. It was drawn up over half a century ago in accordance with the knowl-edge, attitudes, values and modes of practice prevalent at the time. Today both the whalers and conservationists find themselves saddled with an institution that is unable to function effectively. The anti-whalers are frustrated by its lack of conservation muscle, while for the whalers it has failed to 'make possible the orderly development of the whaling industry' as its founders intended. If it were revamped according to modern principles, the ICRW would look very different. Mechanisms to penalise non-compliance would be introduced, bringing it in line with other multilateral environmental agreements. Scientific permits would be issued only on approval of an independent scientific committee, and the produce generated would not be saleable. The decision to kill animals for research would be fully scientifically assessed and ethically reviewed. 'Aboriginal subsistence whaling' would receive a proper definition, along with formal criteria for evaluating quotas, and the organisation's jurisdiction would be expanded to cover all cetaceans. But the ICRW can be revised only if its signatories come to a unanimous agreement, and in the current deadlock this has never looked less likely.

At present the integrity of the IWC is being constantly undermined. As Japan and Norway continue to increase their self-allocated quotas, some members have suggested that the RMP, although fundamentally flawed, may be preferable to an IWC that is so compromised it can no longer function with any authority. If some floating nations do succumb to this notion, the conservationists' worst fears may be realised. The conservationists make a compelling case that in the absence of stringent controls, effective deterrents for rule-breakers, and unequivocal evidence of the restoration of whale populations, the resumption of commercial whaling would be premature. Furthermore, the harpoon is far from the only danger now faced by whales and dolphins. Cetaceans are under immense and escalating pressure from many other sources including habitat loss, noise pollution, commercial fisheries, chemical pollution and climate change, and for these reasons their protection should take precedence over their exploitation.

Over the next few years we will learn whether the energy, expenditure and fierce tenacity of the whalers will lead to the revitalisation of their industry, or whether those who wish to save the whales will carry the day. With both sides having adopted such entrenched partisan positions, it is impossible to imagine that a consensus could ever be reached.

Sharing the sea

On habitat loss, the perils of fishing nets, and noise pollution

WHALES AND DOLPHINS have inhabited the sea for millions of years. Relatively recently, in evolutionary terms, a new species came along and started making use of the world's waters for its own purposes. At first the impact of humans was minor but in the last couple of hundred years it has escalated. The oceans are unimaginably vast, but people still manage to gobble up their resources and degrade their quality at an astounding rate.

Throughout human history the sea has greatly influenced the establishment of settlements, offering an abundance of natural riches and possibilities for trade. Two-thirds of the world's major cities are situated on a coastline or large estuary. It has been estimated that by the year 2050 some 60% of the world's population will be living within 70 km (43 miles) of the coast. Humans, as a species, are not good at sharing and as their exploitation of the oceans continues, whales and dolphins are feeling the squeeze. Burgeoning coastal and riverside communities occupy and degrade the cetaceans' habitat. Less direct, but even more potent, are the impacts of fisheries, shipping and industry. Increasingly dominated by human activity, the seas are busy, noisy and cluttered like never before.

THE HUMAN UTILISATION OF RIVERS, estuaries, coastal zones and marine waters jeopardises the lives of the whales and dolphins that live there. Habitat is eroded and lost through land reclamation, dredging of shipping channels, dumping of spoil, mariculture (fish farms) and the construction of harbours, ports and coastal defences. The untrammelled development of Singapore, for example, has resulted in the destruction of all its mangrove swamps, most of its seagrass beds and all but 5% of its coral reefs.

Unfortunately, damage inflicted on the coastal zone has a disproportionate impact on the wider marine environment. This is because so many of the plants that form the foundation of complex food webs flourish in warm, nutrient-rich coastal waters. Whales and dolphins that live in relatively confined coastal areas are the most vulnerable to habitat loss. However, even some oceanic species, such as humpback and right whales, which spend much of their lives out of range of most human activities, have to move inshore during crucial parts of their life-cycles such as calving.

Some coastal waters are so congested with shipping traffic that collisions have become a major cause of mortality for various species. Fin and sperm whales are routinely struck in the Mediterranean Sea, southern right whale fatalities near Argentina are not uncommon, and vessel collisions are one of the factors that caused New Zealand's Hector's dolphin to become endangered. The North Atlantic right whale faces the greatest problem in this regard. Having been decimated by whalers from the 12th century onwards, it has shown no evidence of recovery despite having received complete protection from hunting since 1935. Many right whales live around busy shipping lanes off the east coast of North America and between 1970 and 2003 at least 29 died after being struck by a vessel. These whales are thought to be particularly susceptible to strikes because they swim in an unhurried fashion, spend considerable time at the surface, and apparently take little or no evasive action when ships bear down on them. It is possible that the whales respond to ships as they do to approaching orcas – by remaining still and silent near the water's surface. Despite efforts to reduce mortality, the population hovers at around 300. Right whales breed exceptionally slowly with females bearing a single calf once every three to five years. With the additional pressure it is under, the North Atlantic right whale faces an uncertain future.

The species most threatened by the destruction of their habitat, however, are the river dolphins. These elusive freshwater creatures, thought to have evolved from marine ancestors, have little in common with their oceanic counterparts today. Three of the world's four true river dolphins (the bhulan or Indus river dolphin, the susu or Ganges river dolphin, and the baiji or Chinese river dolphin) inhabit monsoon-fed rivers in Asia, a region currently undergoing a dynamic economic and industrial growth spurt. The dolphins are forced to compete directly with people for living space, fresh water and food. The Asian river dolphins are all endangered and becoming increasingly scarce as the rivers in which they live are altered and despoiled. People release pollutants into the rivers and draw out fresh water for domestic,

The baiji is probably the most endangered cetacean in the world.

industrial and agricultural use; they kill dolphins purposefully for their meat and accidentally by colliding with them in boats and catching them in fishing nets. But possibly the most harmful alteration to rivers is the construction of dams and barrages. These structures can be lethal for dolphin populations; they cause groups to become isolated from each other, block seasonal migrations and reduce the amount of fish available to eat.

The baiji inhabits the mighty Yangtze river in China. It is not only the rarest of the river dolphins, but is widely regarded as the most endangered cetacean in the world. This reticent, graceful animal with its stocky bluish-grey upper body, pale undersides, beady eyes and long, slender beak lined with peg-like teeth, is on the brink of extinction less than 100 years after it was first described in scientific literature. The Yangtze was once a sparkling clean river, brimming with aquatic life and home to thousands of baiji. Today, with an incredible 300 million people living on its banks and floodplains, the river is heavily industrialised, glutted with pollutants, crammed with boats and overfished. Only a few dozen baiji remain. Large numbers have been killed because they have collided with vessels and propellers, eaten toxic fish, or become impaled on large fish hooks. The construction of the controversial Three Gorges Dam, which spans the Yangtze and is the largest dam in the world, will put further stress on the dwindling baiji population. An attempt to relocate two of the remaining individuals to a semi-natural, protected reserve, was not successful. Although new initiatives are being discussed, some conservationists now believe that the extinction of the Chinese river dolphin is inevitable, and that limited resources would be better directed at other endangered species with greater potential for salvation.

IN THE SHALLOW WATERS of the northernmost section of the Gulf of California, the narrow ribbon of ocean between mainland Mexico and the Baja California peninsula, lives the vaquita. The 'little cow' is a reclusive porpoise distinguished by its tiny size and striking dark patches that encircle its eyes. With around 500 individuals remaining, the vaquita is in serious danger of extinction because of its unfortunate habit of getting caught in fishing nets.

The vaquita is not the only cetacean to die as bycatch – the term used for all non-target animals accidentally caught in fishing nets. It is estimated that over 300,000 whales and dolphins are killed in this way every year, along with countless fish, seabirds, turtles, invertebrates and other marine mammals. The global fishing industry is in fact the greatest human-induced cause of cetacean mortality today. Smaller species, mainly dolphins and porpoises, suffer the heaviest casualties. On becoming trapped in fishing nets they are unable to break free in order to surface and breathe. Drowning in a fishing net is not a peaceful death – injuries sustained during the struggle typically include bruising, muscular tearing, broken beaks, torn and severed fins and flukes, and cuts and abrasions on the skin. Larger whales are more able to free themselves, but they often end up towing sections of broken net wrapped around them, leading to open sores, infections and even death. Entanglement in nets and buoy lines is another major factor in the continued decline of the North Atlantic right whale.

The oceans represent a classic example of "the tragedy of the commons" – the theory that anyone with unregulated access to a shared resource will attempt to plunder its bounty before their competitors can. The historical notion that the seas are the common property of mankind was first formally described in the Freedom of the Seas doctrine published in 1609. It was subsequently codified in laws that allowed anyone the liberty to fish anywhere more than three miles from shore, an area then known as the high seas. In 1994 the United Nations Convention of the Law of the Sea granted each nation control over its territorial waters, extending 12 nautical miles from the shoreline, and an Exclusive Economic Zone, extending 200 miles. With a few exceptions the high seas remain open to all who choose to fish there.

These laws were drawn up as if the supply of fish was inexhaustible. Today many of the world's fisheries are in crisis: the United Nations Food and Agriculture Organisation (FAO) estimates that 75% of fisheries are either fully or overexploited with only the remaining quarter of fish stocks plundered in a sustainable way. With a growing world population, ever-larger fishing vessels and increasingly sophisticated fishing technology, fish are being tracked down and hauled out of the sea in unprecedented numbers. Every year approximately 80 million tonnes of marine life are sieved from the world's oceans. Of this nearly a quarter of the catch, amounting to 20 million tonnes of waste, is thrown back into the sea as bycatch. The bycaught animals are usually rejected because they are under-sized, banned or restricted, have no commercial value, or because the vessel has reached its quota.

The majority of cetacean bycatch occurs in two types of fishing gear: 'passive' gear comprising fixed or drifting nets and traps; and 'towed' nets that are dragged through the water by boats. The vaquita is a victim of a simple, passive fishing gear known as a gillnet. Worldwide, gillnets are the greatest culprits of cetacean bycatch. Sheets of netting are suspended vertically in the water, typically with a line of floats at the top and a lead line weighing down the bottom to keep them more or less upright. On swimming into the net fish become wedged within a mesh opening, or literally 'gilled' by the strands catching behind the gill covers.

Early gillnets were made from natural fibres such as jute or cotton and most cetaceans could either detect them or break free if they did get caught. Their problems started in the 1950s with the advent of synthetic yarns and particularly monofilament netting made of a single strand. These proved extremely popular with fishermen because they were cheap, easy to use, highly productive and very size-selective for fish. But while gillnets allow small fish to escape, they do not discriminate between species – any animal that is equal to or larger than the mesh size can become entangled. Most of the cetaceans that become fatally trapped do so because they are unaware of the nets until it is too late, but sometimes they intentionally forage around the nets and

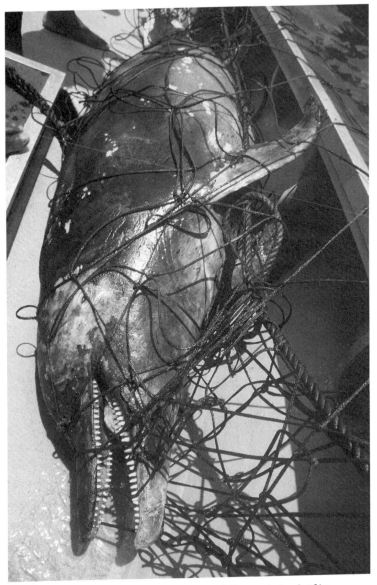

This spotted dolphin became fatally trapped in a fishing net in South Africa.

then accidentally snag a flipper or a fin. A further problem with synthetic gillnets is their durability. When lost at sea, as frequently happens, the non-biodegradable 'ghost nets' can continue 'ghost fishing' indefinitely.

Gillnets can be 'bottom-set' near the sea bed or left to float near the water's surface. Historically, these floating 'driftnets' were short in length and used to catch fish such as sprat and mackerel in coastal waters, but the synthetic revolution led to the development of enormous nets up to 60 km (37 miles) long, which were used to target offshore species including tuna, squid and swordfish. Super-sized driftnets were outlawed globally in 1992, and their length restricted to 2.5 km (1½ miles). The European Union went further and banned driftnets of any length in swordfish and tuna fisheries, but their use by some countries continues – in the last few years Italian fishermen have been illegally deploying large driftnets in the Mediterranean, exacting a deadly toll on whales, dolphins and other marine life.

The hapless vaquita is not the only porpoise with a gillnet problem. Its close relative the harbour porpoise is also prone to fatal capture. In some areas such as the Baltic Sea the harbour porpoise has become critically depleted, but in this case there is greater hope that it can be rescued by enforced political action. In theory the most important legislation protecting whales and dolphins in European waters is the EU Habitats and Species Directive of 1992, under which all cetaceans are strictly protected. The Directive compels EU nations to monitor the incidental capture and killing of cetaceans and stipulates that "in the light of the information gathered, Member States shall take further research or conservation measures as required to ensure that incidental capture and killing does not have significant negative impact on the species concerned". In practice, most countries have failed to fulfil their obligations although some have developed their own regulations at a more local level. The nations that fish in the Baltic Sea banded together and in 2002 produced a plan to save the Baltic harbour porpoise by shifting towards the use of less harmful fishing gear. The EU strengthened the plan with legislation that requires the phasing out and elimination of driftnet fisheries in the Baltic, and the introduction of a new technology known as the pinger in other offending gillnet fisheries. Pingers, or acoustic deterrent devices, are small electronic gadgets attached to nets that emit shrill pulsing sounds designed to alert cetaceans to the presence of the nets. Trials conducted in many parts of the world have demonstrated impressive reductions in cetacean bycatch rates. The Californian gillnet fishery for swordfish and sharks – an industry responsible for capturing numerous short-beaked common dolphins – reported bycatch reductions of two thirds, and a trial off southwest England found that pingers could reduce harbour porpoise catches in gillnets by over 90%.

But pingers are not without their drawbacks. An Argentinean experiment tested their efficacy at reducing the bycatch of Franciscana dolphins by a gillnet fishery. The dolphins stayed away as anticipated, but the fearless local sea lions soon learnt that the pingers indicated an abundant source of trapped, fresh fish – the so-called 'dinner bell' effect – and raced to eat the day's catch. Conservationists also have concerns about their long-term effectiveness. Their widespread deployment may lead to cetaceans shying away from vital habitat where the fish on which they depend are found. It is also possible that cetaceans will become habituated to the 'pinging' and regain confidence around the nets. Enforcement could also be a problem; pingers are expensive, require maintenance such as periodic battery changing, are prone to failure and may interfere with the setting and hauling of nets. For these reasons their use would have to be stringently monitored to ensure compliance.

Another passive fishing practice with a bad bycatch record is longlining. Longline fisheries use a mainline, up to 60 km (37 miles) long, from which dangle thousands of baited hooks. An estimated ten billion longline hooks are deployed around the world every year. They target a number of fish including swordfish and bluefin tuna, but are entirely indiscriminate in what they catch. The longlines have an established reputation for ensnaring sharks, sea turtles and seabirds such as albatross, but they have also been found to injure and kill significant numbers of cetaceans, including Risso's dolphins, common dolphins, pilot whales and false killer whales.

OF THE TOWED FISHING GEARS, the most infamous with regard to cetacean bycatch are the purse-seine nets used to catch highly prized yellowfin tuna off the west coasts of Mexico and Central America. The tuna habitually school underneath objects at the surface including herds of dolphins. No one knows for sure why the fish do this but it is thought they may use the shadows cast by surface objects to hide from predators. In the 1920s American fishermen operating from small vessels realised that they could take advantage of the tuna-dolphin association; they approached the dolphins, flung live bait overboard, whipped the tuna into a feeding frenzy and then plucked them from the sea with hooks.

In the 1950s this small fishery acquired purse-seine nets. Previously the nets had been used to catch only small species like mackerel, but the introduction of hydraulic pumps allowed the nets to be set on larger fish and the fishermen began to exploit the tuna-dolphin association on an industrial scale. The dolphins were chased and corralled into a compact group by speedboats sent out from the main vessel, the purse seiner. The boat then circled the dolphins, unravelling the net that hung deep beneath floats on the ocean's surface, while a small boat called a skiff held one end stationary. The net was then drawn or 'pursed' closed at the bottom, trapping both tuna and dolphins. The panicking dolphins that failed to swim to freedom were either entangled and drowned in the net or crushed as they passed through the winch when the net was hauled. From 1959 onwards over six million dolphins perished in this way. Accounting for 95% of the fatalities were spotted, spinner and common dolphins – gregarious species that form the large pods with which tuna like to associate.

In the early 1970s American fishermen developed two methods which, when used together, proved extremely successful at reducing the numbers of dying dolphins: the 'backing down' procedure and the 'Medina Panel'. With the backing down procedure part of the net's float rope is forced below the surface, creating a channel through which the dolphins can escape. The Medina panel is a small-meshed panel in the area of the net where the backdown occurs, which is less likely to entangle dolphins. Dolphin mortality plummeted and remained at low levels for a decade, but by the early 1980s the USA's tuna fleet had dwindled to only a few boats. As fleets from Latin American and Pacific nations took over, mortality skyrocketed again. Over 120,000 dolphins were killed in 1986 alone. Nothing much was done to remedy the situation until 1987 when video footage of the carnage, filmed by a man employed as a cook on a Panamanian purse seiner, was released. Public outrage ensued and, anxious to avoid consumer boycotts, American tuna canners took action. They started ensuring that their tuna was not caught in association with dolphins, and labelled cans as 'dolphin safe'. These voluntary measures were subsequently backed up by federal legislation.

All vessels of a certain size now use the backdown procedure and Medina panels, after a regional agreement in the early 1990s made these practices universal requirements in the fishery. Although far fewer dolphins are now killed outright as a result, the story does not end there. There is an ongoing battle to maintain the integrity of the American 'dolphin safe' label. Some countries, particularly Mexico, are crusading for the renewed right to catch tuna destined for the American market with nets set on dolphins. They argue that if independent observers testify that no dolphins were killed in the set, the tuna should earn the 'safe' distinction. Conservationists and animal welfare campaigners are up in arms. They fear that the impartiality of observers may be compromised by bribery or intimidation, while the large size of the purse seine nets makes it impossible for a single witness to observe the entire operation. Furthermore, surveys have shown that the depleted dolphin stocks in the region are not recovering as expected. Even if dolphins do not die in the nets it is thought that the chase, which can take up to two hours, and subsequent encirclement, could be causing severe stress and separating vulnerable calves from their mothers.

Another debate rages over the relative merits of alternative methods for catching tuna. The most popular technique is to float and later encircle a buoyant man-made object known as a fish aggregation device. These attract tuna and a multitude of other ocean creatures including vulnerable sharks, rays and sea turtles, all of which are scooped out of the sea together. Many believe that while friendly to dolphins, these tactics threaten a great number of other species and confuse the consumer by earning the tuna canning companies conservation kudos that they may not deserve. The least destructive fishing method overall, according to many conservation groups, is to locate tuna schools swimming independently with fish-finding sonar. Unfortunately, many countries are unwilling to adopt this method because of the extra expense and work involved.

There may be no truly environmentally sound way to catch yellowfin tuna, but the dilemma may soon become academic. As demand for the fish's tasty flesh continues to rise, industrial fishing activity in the region is expanding. In 2003 regional experts warned that unless urgent action is taken, the tuna population is likely to begin crashing within five years. If that happens the fleets will move on, leaving an emptier ocean behind them.

There is another towed fishing system, pelagic trawling, that regularly kills large numbers of dolphins, although it receives less public attention than purse seine operations. It involves the towing of a bag net either by a single boat (single trawl) or strung between two boats (pair trawl). The nets have wide mouths that gradually taper to a narrow tube called the extension piece, which leads to the cod-end, the closed end of the net where the fish are collected. The nets are vast – a pair trawl net for mackerel fishing has a mouth opening of up to $60 \times 120\,\text{m}$ ($200 \times 400\,\text{ft}$), can be $1.6\,\text{km}$ ($1\,\text{mile}$) long, and spacious enough to accommodate the Sydney Opera House. Weights and floats keep the mouth gaping open as the net cruises through the water, consuming everything in its path.

Pelagic trawls are widely used by a number of countries despite their voracity and lack of discrimination. In the northeast Atlantic European trawlers, mostly fishing in pairs, target a medley of fish species including albacore tuna, hake, herring, mackerel, horse mackerel, sea bass, pilchard and anchovy. Along with their target species the nets engulf hordes of common dolphins and Atlantic white-sided dolphins, and smaller numbers of striped dolphins, bottlenose dolphins and long-finned pilot whales. Information on mortality rates is patchy, but hundreds of dead dolphins sporting injuries consistent with a frantic struggle in a fishing net wash up on beaches in the UK, Ireland and France every year. Since the majority of carcasses sink out at sea, the true annual death toll is feared to be as great as 10,000.

Researchers are experimenting with ways to adapt the nets in the hope of preventing the deaths of so many dolphins in pelagic trawls. They have developed nets that incorporate a metal 'separator grid' placed in the extension piece and angled to deflect large animals up to an escape hatch, while fish carry on through to the cod-end. Preliminary trials indicated that the grids work although some of the dolphins swam back out of the net rather than up through the escape hatch as anticipated. It is possible that they detected the grid and were discouraged from venturing too far in. But, as with all technical developments, the necessary trials and modifications are a slow and expensive business. At the end of the day, no matter how successful any bycatch reduction method may prove to be, it is unlikely to be widely adopted by cost-conscious commercial fisheries unless its use is enforced through legislation.

WHEN HUMANS MAKE USE of the sea they tend to produce a lot of noise. The ocean has always been a noisy place. Before humans started adding to the underwater clamour, natural sounds predominated, from the winds that whisk the surface water to the volcanoes and earthquakes that rent the seabed. In the rocky areas of tropical and temperate seas, snapping shrimp and other invertebrates generate a constant sizzling hum, in polar seas colliding icebergs and floes rumble and roar, in coastal waters shifting sediments smash and grind while cetaceans, seals and the more vocal fishes all make their own contributions to the underwater hubbub.

Though the deep ocean is full of sound, it is almost devoid of light. Sound travels through water with amazing efficiency, five times faster and many times further than in air. Light, conversely, transmits poorly through water and does not penetrate far below the ocean surface. For cetaceans that swim at great depths the only light comes from the intermittent glows and sparkling flashes of bioluminescent species of jellyfish, squid and fish. So as well as having relatively good vision, whales and dolphins have developed a superb sense of hearing. This probably allows them to 'hear' their environment with as much detail and clarity as humans see theirs, and enables them to navigate and hunt in the inky depths of the sea.

This remarkable ability developed long ago in evolutionary history. As the ancestors of modern cetaceans became true denizens of the ocean, their sensory systems underwent a radical overhaul. Hearing soon became the most important of the five senses. The way cetacean hearing works reflects the fact that it mostly takes place underwater. 'Ears' comprise an inner, middle and outer section. In whales and dolphins, the canals of the outer ears are plugged. Rather than entering the ear directly from the environment, most sound is channelled to the bones of the middle ear along special tissues in and around the lower jawbone. The bones of the middle ear are not fused to the skull, as they are in terrestrial mammals, but instead are suspended in a cavity filled with a foamy, sponge-like substance. This isolates the bones, acoustically, from sound conducted through the skull bones. Consequently, most sound arrives via the tissues near the jawbone, and this enables the animal to determine the position of the sound's source. This is essential for creatures that understand their watery world primarily by listening to it.

Whales and dolphins depend on sound in all aspects of their lives. With their sophisticated hearing they hunt for food, detect

Common dolphins off the coast of Gibraltar are bombarded by man-made noise.

predators such as orcas and sharks, and navigate epic migratory routes. By calling to each other, members of the same species identify themselves, create and maintain social bonds, find prospective mates, establish territories and keep the herd together.

The main properties of sound are loudness or intensity, measured in decibels (dB), and frequency or pitch, expressed in hertz (Hz). Cetaceans employ the broadest acoustic range of any mammal group. Dolphins produce high-frequency whistles, squeaks and clicks either singly, in bursts, or in a continuous stream. Like all other toothed whales, they also rely on sound for echolocation, which they use to create a mental map of their environment and hunt prey. An echolocating odontocete generates intense bursts of high-frequency noise (3000–120,000 Hz) in a region of soft tissue associated with the blow-hole on top of the head. The sound, transmitted as a narrow beam, bounces off an object and returns as an echo, providing the animal with detailed information about the physical features of its surroundings.

Baleen whales do not echolocate but still use sound to monitor their environment and communicate. They produce big, booming, low-frequency moans, bellows, snorts and grunts. Some species may be able to broadcast their calls over thousands of kilometres by using an oceanic layer known as the 'deep sound channel'. This is a natural duct along which acoustics are enhanced and its depth varies with water temperature. Like the blue whale, the fin whale produces sounds below 100 Hz at the lower limit of human hearing. Its mating call is heard with such ubiquity in some areas that for many years it was mistaken for the creaking of the ocean floor. The call of the blue whale, at 160–188 dB, is the loudest sound produced by any animal, but even the mightiest of whales is as quiet as a mouse when compared with some of the noises that humans have added to the ocean cacophony in recent times.

Man-made, or anthropogenic, noise has increased massively over the last century as commercial, industrial and recreational maritime activities have expanded. It now poses a serious threat to the well-being and even the survival of all whales and dolphins. Though the dangers of many other forms of pollution have been recognised for decades, scientists and conservationists have only recently started addressing the potential consequences of these unprecedented sound levels. Shipping is the most substantial and pervasive source of man-made noise. Around 150 years ago, when even the largest vessels were wind-powered, the sea was a significantly quieter place. Now, with the introduction of both the powered engine and a growing global economy, more goods are moved around the world by ship than ever before. Noise emanates from a ship's whirring propeller, bellowing engine, rattling bearings, and from the passage of the hull through the water. Larger vessels generally make more noise than smaller ones; supertankers top the scale with their 200 dB roar.

Seismic exploration, used to detect deposits of fossil fuels, is another very powerful sound source. A ship towing an array of airguns fires off thousands of blasts that are intense enough to reflect off layers of rock deep beneath the sea floor. These reflected sounds are analysed to reveal the geological structures below. The blasts produce a more or less constant barrage of noise; a large airgun array can generate sounds over 250 dB and operations often run around the clock. Once oil or gas reserves have been found, additional noise is generated by the increased boat traffic, construction of platforms, laying of pipes and drilling of holes into the bedrock, all to create a complex of industrial structures which, when obsolete, are usually dismantled and removed – noisily. Adding to the relentless ambient din are the sounds produced by the dredging of sea beds, mineral mining, pingers on fishing nets, recreational watersports and sonar.

It is hardly surprising that cetacean ears, which are adapted to be exquisitely sensitive to noise, are also vulnerable to being damaged by it. Whales and dolphins are thought to be especially susceptible to noise pollution because compared to other animals in the sea they are highly developed and depend heavily on sound. It is thought that adding alien and often very powerful sound to their environment has an impact that is comparable, in human terms, to that of very bright lights. Just as humans can be 'blinded' by light beams, so sound can effectively 'blind' whales and dolphins.

Different species are more sensitive to different frequencies and it is assumed that, at the very least, cetaceans are sensitive to the frequencies of their own vocalisations; hence, large cetaceans are affected by low frequencies and small cetaceans by higher ones. Man-made noise is predominantly low frequency, in the band below 1000 Hz, so the species most greatly disturbed by it are the larger whales. As a general rule, the closer the animal is to the source of a noise, the greater its impact is likely to be. Sound radiates outwards from its source, gradually decreasing in power as it spreads like the ripples created by a pebble dropped in a pond. In recent years, the dangers of noise pollution have been highlighted by a series of tragic incidents in which large numbers of whales and dolphins have washed up dead and dying on shore.

The stranding of cetaceans is not a new, or rare, phenomenon. Every year, thousands of cetaceans are found beached on coastlines around the world. Toothed whales strand more frequently than baleen whales and sometimes in their hundreds. Perhaps unsurprisingly, the most prolific mass stranders — sperm whales,

Long-finned pilot whales stranded on the coast of Cape Cod, 1902.

pilot whales and false killer whales – all live in large groups with strong social structures and individuals that act as herd leaders. In these circumstances, should the leader make a mistake and swim ashore, the rest will follow.

The reasons behind these perplexing, seemingly suicidal incidents are still a bit of a mystery. The animals may have ventured too near the coast while pursuing prey or fleeing predators; they may have become trapped or disoriented by rapidly ebbing tides, strong currents or freak weather conditions; or they may be suffering from a debilitating infectious disease. Although stranding can occur anywhere, higher rates are recorded in areas with long, sloping, sandy beaches including parts of New Zealand and Cape Cod in the USA. It is thought that the soft sediments may send back confusing signals to echolocating whales, causing them to lose their way and run aground. Yet another hypothesis rests on the possibility that cetaceans use the Earth's geomagnetic field to navigate. Small quantities of magnetite – a compound that can sense a magnetic field – have been detected in the brain and skull of some species. An analysis of strandings around the UK coast found that they occur most frequently on those unusual shores where lines of equal magnetic force meet the coastline at a 90° angle. It is possible that the beached animals were misled by these abnormalities and followed them into land.

Most strandings involve a single species but many of the events triggered by noise pollution have involved multiple species, a sure sign that some kind of catastrophic incident has taken place out at sea. In 1996, 12 Cuvier's beaked whales, a species that rarely strands, washed up dead on the coast of Greece. In 2000, 13 beaked whales and two minke whales stranded in the Bahamas and two years later, a group of 14 animals, containing three species of beaked whale, beached on the Canary Islands. What all these bizarre incidents had in common was that they had occurred shortly after the navies of various countries had conducted experiments or training exercises involving sonar in the area.

Navies use sonar to detect the presence of submarines. The first military sonars were passive; they emitted no sound but merely listened for enemy vessels. By the end of the First World War active sonars had been developed. These transmit a sound and listen for the echo that bounces off a target. As the cold war gained momentum during the 1960s, the Soviet Navy developed submarines that were much stealthier and harder to pinpoint. The US Navy responded by introducing a new generation of active sonars to detect and track them. Sweeping the ocean with sonic blares up to 235 dB in strength, these mid-range active sonars could pose a serious danger to cetaceans and other marine animals that are exposed to them.

In all the suspect stranding incidents, autopsies conducted on the dead cetaceans found no disease or physical abnormality. However, the animals that stranded in the Bahamas were bleeding from the ears – a form of damage that could have been caused by sonar – and those on the Canary Islands revealed lesions in vital organs and unusual bubbles of gas and fat in body tissues. The scientists examining these corpses realised that the whales had probably suffered from something like 'the bends', otherwise known as decompression sickness, which can affect deep-sea diving humans but was previously thought an impossible condition in whales. Precisely how this came about is not known, but it is most likely that the sonar caused the animals to swim to the surface too rapidly and stay there, rather than diving again.

Now a possibly greater threat to cetaceans is emerging. The navies of the USA and a number of European countries including the UK are developing and deploying a new class of active sonar. Operating in a low-frequency bandwidth, it can bombard much greater areas of ocean with noise. It is so powerful that at a range of 160 km (100 miles) the signal could still reach 160 dB.

In 2003 conservation and animal welfare organisations mounted a successful legal challenge that placed restrictions on the US Navy's low-frequency sonar programme, limiting its use to the waters of the western North Pacific during peace time. Its mid-range sonar initiatives are also being challenged in the courts. Across the Atlantic, the European Parliament voted, in 2004, in favour of a moratorium on the use of naval sonar pending the completion of an environmental impact survey to ascertain the effects of the noise on cetaceans, other marine mammals and fish. Unfortunately, this reprieve is proving fairly meaningless. Although some safety measures have been put in place, their efficacy is unproven and they are considered inadequate by many campaigners. Furthermore, low-frequency sound technology is being utilised by another scientific enterprise known as acoustic thermometry. On the premise that sound moves faster in warm water than cold, researchers plan to monitor changes in average ocean temperatures by measuring the number of seconds a powerful signal takes to travel from its source to a specified destination. If the transmissions gain speed over time, this would provide evidence for the effects of global warming. Given the variability of local climate, only great lengths of water will suffice, so the signal is directed down the ocean's natural deep sound channel – the same one which blue, fin and other whales use to communicate with each other over vast distances. They, along with sperm whales and the various deep-diving beaked whales that regularly descend hundreds or even thousands of metres, are thought to be at risk, while animals swimming higher in the water column could be affected by sound that breaks towards the surface.

The death of an animal as a direct result of noise pollution is the most extreme and dramatic possible consequence. Further from the sound source the injuries sustained are more subtle. Whales and dolphins can suffer from deafness because the sensitivity of hair cells within the inner ear is reduced. These delicate structures communicate differences in loudness and pitch to the brain and are easily damaged. Hearing loss may be temporary or permanent, depending on the intensity and duration of the noise to which the animal is exposed, but temporary deafness will eventually become permanent if the noise persists. Given the extent to which whales and dolphins rely on hearing, deafness can significantly affect their chances of survival. In one recorded incident two sperm whales, a mature female and a male calf, were struck and killed by a cargo ship while resting at the surface. Neither whale had made any attempt to move out of the path of the oncoming vessel. The post-mortem reports revealed that both animals had damaged inner ears – they had been rendered deaf by heavy local shipping traffic.

Additionally, man-made noises can drown out natural noises – a phenomenon known as masking. During their breeding season male humpback whales sing complex songs consisting of low grunts, squeals, chirps, whistles and wails organised into distinct themes that are thought to be a form of sexual display. When exposed to loud masking noises, the whales compensate by singing for longer. For widely dispersed species such as fin and blue whales the masking of long-range mating calls could have dire consequences. If females cannot hear calling males it could cut down encounter rates in animals that are already endangered and breed very slowly.

Whales and dolphins typically respond to noise by swimming quickly away from it and making lengthy dives. Gray whales have been shown to alter their highly predictable migration passages in order to avoid sounds of 120 dB, and in the Canadian high Arctic, beluga whales and their close relatives, narwhals, react to approaching ice-breaking ships from up to 80 km (50 miles) away. While belugas flee far from their original position, narwhals tend to freeze and huddle into a tight pod. These behaviours mirror the ways both species typically respond to predatory orcas. Although these impacts might seem trivial, the combined effects of more swimming and diving and less feeding are likely to impinge on the health and reproductive success of cetacean populations. This particularly applies to those species that do not carry much 'spare' energy, and to vulnerable individuals such as young calves and nursing mothers. Exposure to noise can also lead to elevated levels of stress, the pervasive effects of which are well known.

With noise levels in the ocean continually rising action needs to be taken before they reach a crescendo that seriously compromises cetaceans and other forms of marine life. To date far more is known about the sources of undersea noise than about its effects. The public profile of noise pollution remains relatively low and it receives little attention from policy makers. Efforts to combat noise pollution are hampered because the science to be applied is sketchy, and the size and complexity of the industries that would be affected by regulation are formidable. Logical measures to eliminate unnecessary noise include obligatory environmental assessments of all noise-producing industrial and military procedures, the promotion of boats designed to be quieter, data-sharing systems for seismic surveyors (to avoid the repeated surveying of the same area, as frequently happens), and the employment of mitigation measures, such as 'soft start' procedures, to encourage animals to leave the area.

Greater political action will be needed to save cetaceans from dying in fishing nets and being deafened by man-made noise. As incidences of bycatch are often attributed to fishing fleets from several countries, and both whales and sound pass through different nations' marine territories and the high seas, legislation must be made and implemented by international bodies. More data needs to be gathered and workable solutions should be developed and tested. In addition to technical fixes, local and seasonal restrictions on fishing and noise-creating activities that correspond to the presence of high concentrations of whales and dolphins can make a big difference. These measures are urgently required to prevent an irreversible tragedy of the commons.

Hot water and heavy metals

On climate change and chemical pollution

Human activity is changing the very nature of the planet. The largest population in history, with its modern technology and patterns of consumption, is bringing about extensive alterations to the Earth's climate, atmosphere and oceans. For whales and dolphins the changes with the most profound implications are global warming, which is driving an increase in sea temperatures, and chemical pollution of their marine environment. There is little consensus on the scale of the damage and its long-term ramifications, but the consequences for cetaceans are potentially devastating.

In 1999 and 2000 alarming numbers of emaciated gray whales were found dead in the North Pacific Ocean. Their starving condition was a consequence of global warming; sea surface temperatures had risen and the tiny crustaceans on which the whales depend had failed to prosper. Of all human modifications to the planet, climate change is the most complicated. It is impossible to make accurate predictions about the future. As the numerous interacting variables give rise to wildly different forecasts the scientific debate, along with the climate, is heating up. The scientific study of when and how climate change will affect whales and dolphins is also in its infancy and there is a dearth of hard evidence. Scientists are forced to speculate and make the best possible predictions by creating models and theoretical scenarios. It is important that they do so because climate change looks set to transform the planet, and for whales and dolphins it might prove the greatest threat of all.

Climate change is not a new phenomenon and neither is global warming. Over its five billion year history the Earth has repeatedly warmed up and cooled down. During some periods balmy seas and steamy jungles dominated; during others landmasses became bleak arid deserts and the polar ice sheets extended to cover southern Australia and parts of North America and Europe. The difference this time is that the climate appears to be changing as a direct result of human activities, and it is changing fast.

Before the Industrial Revolution the atmospheric concentration of carbon dioxide – the most important of the 'greenhouse gases' – was 270 parts per million (ppm). Since then, the level has soared to 360 ppm, largely as a consequence of the burning of fossil fuels. Average temperatures around the world have risen by approximately 0.6°C (1.1°F) in the last 150 years. The Intergovernmental Panel on Climate Change (IPCC), the largest and most important body dedicated to climate change science, has predicted a total rise of 1.4–5.8°C (2.5–10.4°F) above 1900 levels by the end of the 21st century. Evidence to support their position is mounting but the climate of the future still remains shrouded in mystery. Uncertainty stems from the convoluted relationships between different planetary processes such as wind patterns, ocean circulation, and the formation of ice and clouds in the atmosphere. Their interactions might exacerbate the warming effect or, as some climate change sceptics believe, actually dampen it down.

There is already compelling evidence of the repercussions of climate change. A study by NASA declared 2005 to have been the warmest year on record. The recent scorching heatwaves in Europe, unusually forceful hurricanes in the Americas, and torrential floods and storms in Africa may be a taste of what's to come. In Europe trees flower, insects emerge and birds lay their eggs earlier, some growing-seasons are longer, glaciers and mountain snows are melting, and cold-sensitive butterflies, beetles and dragonflies have moved their ranges northwards.

The effects of climate change on marine ecosystems are especially hard to predict because of the complex interactions between climate and ocean processes. The ocean soaks up some of the heat generated by global warming and there is evidence that over the last 50 years the deep ocean has become slightly warmer – by 0.06°C (0.11°F) – while shallower waters have heated up somewhat more – by 0.31°C (0.56°F). Global warming also triggers changes in ocean circulation and salinity and reduces the amount of sea-ice cover at the poles. With a hotter global climate sea levels rise, the marine concentration of carbon dioxide increases, there are more storms, stronger winds and choppier seas.

As the case of the famished North Pacific gray whales demonstrates, the most severe impact of climate change on whales and dolphins is likely to be its influence on their prey. The distribution of plankton, squid and fish is greatly influenced by temperature. Although whales and dolphins roam throughout the world's oceans, they are not evenly spaced; they congregate where

Gray whales could go hungry as a consequence of global warming.

they can find the most food. Marine life thrives around naturally occurring upwellings of nutrient-rich water, and changes to these areas will have the greatest impact on cetacean populations.

The lives of toothed whales are tied to food sources year-round and many species are limited to waters of a certain temperature. Scientists have observed that the warming of the North Sea has prompted the shift of plankton and fish communities northwards towards colder waters. The toothed whales that rely on these food sources are forced to follow them. What impact these population movements will have on different species remains to be seen.

Most baleen whales are less fussy about water temperatures because their long seasonal migrations acclimatise them to a great range. The retreat of the polar ice may, however, cause problems for species such as gray and humpback whales that migrate tremendous distances. If the whales have to travel farther to reach the ice edge, where the densest concentrations of prey are found, they will spend more energy swimming and have less time available for eating. Underfed whales will not reproduce successfully. Female fin whales produce a calf every year in good conditions, but only every third year in times of relative famine. It is thought that ovulation is suppressed if the whale does not carry sufficient weight or body fat. Similarly, highly endangered North Atlantic right whale calves are much more likely to die during the first few months of life following slumps in availability of their favoured crustacean prey.

Some researchers are investigating the impact of extreme weather events, such as El Niño, as a proxy for climate change. These events, which trigger wide-ranging changes to ocean ecosystems, may anticipate the 'normal' conditions of the future. The frequency and severity of El Niño events have increased over the last 30 years and global warming could further exacerbate them. During the 1982/83 event bottlenose dolphins living offshore near southern California expanded their range northwards, presumably in response to a shift in prey distribution. At the same time vast shoals of market squid vanished from the region, leading to an absence of the short-finned pilot whales that usually feast on them. When the squid eventually returned, pods of Risso's dolphin followed in their wake. It is thought they were taking advantage of the vacant niche created by climatic disruption.

TEMPERATURES ARE SPIRALLING upwards at the poles and it is at the ends of the Earth that global warming will most profoundly affect whales and dolphins. As countless images of forlorn polar bears huddled on shrinking ice floes testify, the situation in the Arctic is fast becoming critical. The Arctic is warming almost twice as fast as most of the planet, and temperatures have risen by 3–4°C (5–7°F) in only 50 years. The sea ice is retreating at around 8% per decade. As the ice sheet melts, the warming process accelerates because the exposed dark water absorbs heat from the sun that was previously reflected back into space by the brilliant white ice. If current trends continue the Arctic might be ice-free before the end of the 21st century.

Vast, verdant mats of emerald green algae flourish beneath the sea ice. This plant life forms the foundation of the entire Arctic food web and without it the three Arctic whales – the bowhead, beluga and narwhal – will suffer. The algae support innumerable tiny animal plankton, which are consumed in vast quantities by the bowhead. The plankton are also eaten by Arctic cod and other fish on which the beluga and narwhal prey.

The bowhead follows the continual advance and retreat of the ice edge. It passes the long, cold winter in total darkness with very little to eat, but come the summer its world is illuminated by 24 hour sunshine and the ice breaks up. The whales penetrate cracks and leads, pushing as far north as they can before the great winter freeze sets in and drives them back south. During the bowhead's evolutionary history the Arctic climate periodically warmed and cooled. As the extent and shape of the ice cover shifted, so the adaptable whales altered their migratory routes to keep themselves close to the ice edge. But the Arctic is being transformed much more rapidly than the bowhead is accustomed to. It is not known whether it will be able to adopt new migration routes and feeding grounds quickly enough to keep up. This concern applies to many cetaceans. Like most marine mammals, whales and dolphins show considerable behavioural plasticity – they can mould their activities in response to environmental changes. But the limits of their flexibility are not known. They have adapted to momentous climate change many times through their long history, but the present changes are taking place within a mere half century. This equates to the average lifespan of a single whale, leaving them little time to adapt or evolve.

Another outcome of the Arctic thaw is the unsealing of the Northwest Passage, the perilous ice-clogged shipping route running along the top of Canada and Alaska. Open water for at least some of the year could expose the beleaguered Arctic whales to increased shipping traffic and industrial activity, with an accompanying escalation in noise pollution and the risk of oil spills. Meanwhile, the melting ice sheets will flood the sea with fresh water and reduce ocean salinity, further disrupting essential food webs.

On the other side of the globe warming is occurring at a comparable rate. Antarctica is the feeding ground of 90% of the world's remaining great whales. Krill, the small shrimp-like crustaceans that swarm in dense clouds in the open ocean, provide a summer banquet for blue, fin, sei, humpback and minke whales,

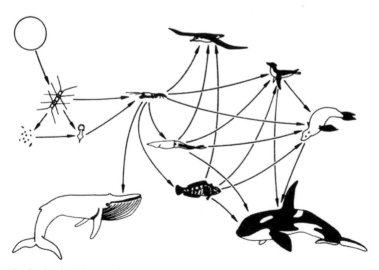

The food web of the Southern Ocean.

as well as penguins, albatrosses and seals. Krill graze on plant plankton that bloom every spring under the ice. Where the sea ice recedes, krill populations falter. Taking their place are thriving communities of salps — semi-transparent, gelatinous, barrel-shaped marine animals that resemble small jellyfish. Salps are more tolerant of warmer, nutrient-poor water and it is thought that their range is expanding at the expense of the krill. The problem for whales is that they do not eat salps. Instead, they rely on a predictable and plentiful supply of krill.

The Southern Ocean food chain is further jeopardised by the infamous hole in the ozone layer. Essential to life as we know it, ozone shields the Earth from some 99% of the harmful UV-B radiation emitted by the Sun. The general thinning of the ozone

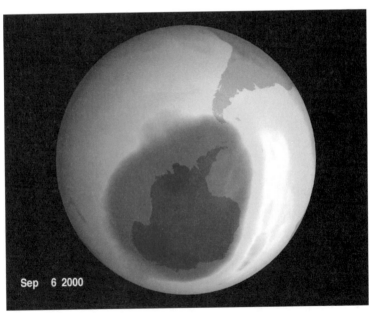

September 2000: the hole in the ozone layer is the dark grey zone that stretches across the landmass of Antarctica to the tip of South America.

layer and the hole were first discovered in the mid 1980s. The phenomenon is a consequence of the introduction of various chemicals to the atmosphere, the most abundant of which is chlorine. Chlorine atoms set off a chain of reactions that allow each one to destroy up to 100,000 ozone molecules. Ozone depletion is dangerous because the extra radiation will intensify global warming and is harmful to living things. UV-B radiation has been shown to reduce plant yields, debilitate animals, and cause skin cancers, cataracts and weakened immune systems in humans. Whales and dolphins seem less vulnerable because most have darkly pigmented skin and spend much of their time in the ocean depths, out of reach of the blistering rays. However, the elevated radiation could be stunting the growth of marine plankton, causing a knock-on effect in the food chain.

The largest ever hole, measuring 28.4 million km^2 (11 million sq miles) – three times the land area of the USA – was recorded during the 2000/1 season. While no hole has appeared elsewhere, the ozone layer over the Arctic has been shown to thin by up to 30% during the spring. Following the establishment of the Montreal Protocol in 1987, the production and use of chemicals that harm the ozone layer have been greatly reduced. However, it is thought that the ozone hole will persist until 2010 and that it may take another 50 years before conditions return to normal and the inhabitants of Antarctica are once again shielded from the Sun's obliterating power.

ALTHOUGH THE WORLD'S OCEANS contain an almost unimaginable quantity of water, their capacity is not infinite. The deluge of pollution they absorb every day is diluted, but not to a negligible degree. A significant proportion of what ends up in the sea poses a danger to marine life. Many of the world's cetaceans swim in a toxic soup and, inevitably, are suffering as a result.

Mountains of rubbish enter the oceans, mainly from land sources, at a rate of six million tonnes a year. In one study conducted along the coast of Florida, plastic bags, plastic jugs, disposable surgical gloves and nylon fishing lines were retrieved from the stomachs of dead bottlenose dolphins, false killer whales and a pygmy sperm whale. Smaller items may be of little consequence but larger ones may irritate, puncture or block the gastrointestinal tract, causing sudden death or slow starvation. Inadequate rubbish disposal is also creating unexpected problems for southern right whales. The kelp gull population in Argentina's Península Valdés has boomed, nurtured by waste from local fish processing plants that is left to rot in the open. The aggressive gulls have recently developed the habit of feeding

A kelp gull takes a bite of southern right whale.

on live whales; they land on the animals' backs and gouge out pieces of skin and blubber, creating chains of lesions. The whales respond by flinching violently and fleeing underwater while the gulls circle and wait for them to resurface. Females with calves are now spending about a quarter of the day escaping their tormentors, depleting precious blubber reserves. There is little food available on the nursery grounds so the mothers cannot recoup the energy needed to support their calves' growth, development and migration to their feeding grounds later in the year.

Perhaps the most familiar and most striking of all forms of marine pollution is oil. The worst oil disasters attract widespread media attention but in reality the quantity of pollutants entering the sea this way is completely dwarfed by the amounts that seep in quietly, unseen and unreported. They originate from a range of sources including domestic sewage, industrial discharge, mining, leakage from waste tips, agricultural run-off and atmospheric fallout. The deadliest pollutants of all are completely invisible.

The orcas that cruise the North Pacific, near Washington State and British Columbia on the west coasts of the USA and Canada respectively, are among the most contaminated mammals in the world. Popularly known as a killer whale on account of its predatory habits, the orca is in fact a dolphin – the largest in existence. Its striking piebald appearance – black back, white underside, grey saddle patch, long black flippers, towering dorsal fin and characterful white eye patch – make it instantly recognisable. Towards the end of the 20th century, the death rate of the west coast orcas soared. Animals of all ages seemed equally vulnerable. Scientists investigated the problem by conducting biopsies on living animals and found that they were awash with a highly poisonous family of industrial chemicals called poly-chlorinated biphenyls (PCBs). PCBs were invented in the 1930s

Orcas in the northeast Pacific carry record-breaking contaminant loads.

for use in the manufacture of electrical equipment. Some 40 years later their toxicity was recognised and they were banned in the USA and Canada. But PCBs have an incredibly long lifespan. As the old equipment that contains them reaches the end of its useful life and is disposed of, the chemicals leak into the environment. Carried by air and water, many PCBs find their final resting place on the ocean floor. Some Asian countries still produce PCBs and continue to add to the chemical pile-up in the North Pacific. It takes only a week for airborne contaminants from China to reach the USA.

Since the Industrial Revolution human activity has not only intensified the release of naturally occurring substances, such as carbon dioxide, but it has also introduced numerous chemicals that are entirely foreign to nature. PCBs are organochlorines, a class of highly durable compounds that includes many pesticides. The most infamous of these is DDT, a pesticide that was widely used from 1939 onwards and caused untold damage to wildlife before its pernicious side-effects were identified. Organochlorines do not generally kill animals directly but they cause a roster of horrific health problems. They disrupt hormones, hamper reproduction, damage developing foetuses, promote cancer and weaken the immune system. Without strong immune systems whales and dolphins are vulnerable to rampaging infectious diseases. These are sometimes responsible for mass mortalities known as 'die offs'. Between June 1987 and March 1988 more than 740 bottlenose dolphins living off the east coast of the USA died, reducing the stock by 53%. Then between 1990 and 1992 an epidemic killed over 1000 striped dolphins in the western Mediterranean. The casualties suffered from pneumonia, fever and neurological disorders thought to have been triggered by a harmful viral agent known as a morbillivirus. Autopsies revealed that many of the victims of both outbreaks bore high levels of toxins, particularly PCBs. But although there is little doubt that PCBs are implicated at some level, a direct connection has not yet been proven. Many of the victims lost considerable weight through the course of their illnesses and the depletion of blubber had a concentrating effect on their stock of persistent chemicals, contributing to the high levels registered.

In the case of the North American orcas, PCBs may be rendering them vulnerable to disease and preventing them from breeding successfully. PCBs spread through the food chain from the bottom up, 'biomagnifying' en route from plankton to predator. As top predators, orcas accumulate high concentrations of toxins from their contaminated prey. As long-lived animals – male orcas can survive 45 years while females have been known to attain a venerable 85 – they are especially vulnerable as individuals add to their toxin load throughout their lives. Organochlorines dissolve more readily in fat than water so they accumulate in fatty tissues including the blubber, liver and brain. Females unwittingly divest themselves of much of their toxic cargo by passing it onto their firstborn calves via their high-fat breastmilk. Unfortunately the baby whales are particularly sensitive to the impact of the toxins. The chemicals compromise the young animals' future health by disrupting the hormones that control the development of the immune system, brain, vital organs and reproductive systems.

There are two types of coastal orca in North America: 'residents' and 'transients'. The groups are genetically distinct, eat different prey, communicate with distinct vocal dialects and never mingle. The transients live in family pods of between one and seven animals and it is they who have been identified as possibly the most contaminated mammals in the world. Their diet consists primarily of seals and sea lions. As prolific predators of fish, the seals and sea lions deliver highly concentrated toxin loads to the whales. The resident orcas live in larger social groups of between ten and 60 animals and eat mainly Chinook salmon. Their prey is lower down the food chain and so the orcas acquire fewer contaminants. The 'southern' resident pods, which journey from Canada's west coast through the heavily industrialised Puget Sound in Washington State and on to California's Monterey Bay, carry far heavier toxic burdens than their northern neighbours, which almost never venture into the Sound. As well as the PCBs, it is thought that a decline in salmon combined with a massive increase in whale-watching vessels may also be contributing to the orcas' failing health. These three factors, which together put strain on the orca populations, present a serious challenge for governments and other stakeholders in both Canada and the USA.

Organochlorines are not the only potent toxins that bioaccumulate. Toxins produced by algae, often referred to as "harmful algal blooms", are increasing worldwide. It seems likely that these blooms are promoted by the unnaturally high levels of nutrients and minerals that are introduced to coastal waters from sewage and fertilisers washed out to sea from the land. Global climate change and overfishing of algae-eating fish species may be exacerbating the problem. Like organochlorines, the poisonous compounds released by harmful algae accumulate in ever-greater concentrations as they move up the food chain. In 1987, 14 humpback whales in Cape Cod Bay, off the east coast of the USA, died after eating Atlantic mackerel that were riddled with saxitoxin, a neurotoxin produced by algae that can cause respiratory paralysis even in tiny quantities. From August 1999 to February 2000, 120 dead bottlenose dolphins appeared along the shores of the Florida panhandle. Subsequent post mortems indicated that their deaths were linked to a bloom of the colourful algae responsible for 'red tides'.

Another family of chemicals has wrought havoc in Canada's St Lawrence River. In the 1980s and 1990s beluga whales were found dead on its shores, perplexing locals and scientists alike. Most of the world's 150,000 or so belugas inhabit the frozen expanses of the Arctic Ocean, but a few are found in very cold rivers like the St Lawrence. Of a population numbering around 1200, about 15 animals are found dead every year. In 1983 a team from Montreal University decided to investigate and since then have carried out autopsies on over 100 dead whales. Their findings are shocking: 27% of the adult whales had died of cancer. The whales also hosted a range of non-cancerous tumours and numerous opportunistic viruses and infections. The cancers found in the St Lawrence belugas represent an astonishing 40% of all the cancers ever identified in cetaceans worldwide. The pathologies show great variety – there are cancers of the intestine, stomach, mammary glands, ovaries, uterus and skin. Furthermore, none of the living females over 21 years of age seems to be reproducing successfully although their Arctic cousins, which live to about 35, keep on breeding their whole lives.

The scientists discovered that as well as carrying copious quantities of PCBs, other organochlorines and heavy metals, the whales had been exposed to a group of poisons known as polycyclic aromatic hydrocarbons (PAHs). These noxious chemicals are produced by the incomplete combustion of carbon-containing materials. They are among the carcinogens found in cigarette smoke. The PAHs originate from a large complex of aluminium smelters situated 100 km (62 miles) upstream on the shores of the Saguenay River. After being released into the atmosphere the PAHs collect in river sediments and are ingested by worms. The worms are eaten by belugas, which feed by diving down to the riverbed to forage. The aluminium companies claim that there is no proof that PAHs are killing beluga whales, but scientists have found evidence to the contrary. Twenty kg (44 lb) of worms collected from the Saguenay sediments contained a greater amount of PAHs than a human adult could ingest daily without incurring a high risk of cancer.

The whales are not the only victims – the incidence of human cancer in the area is unusually high by Canadian standards and some of those cancers have been directly linked to the presence of PAHs. Initiatives to restrict the use of harmful substances and remove organochlorines from the river are starting to improve the belugas' lot, but while the aluminium smelters continue to pump out PAHs, the whales remain in grave danger.

Some sources of pollution have been brought under control by international legislation, with commitments to phase out a number of persistent organic pollutants including PCBs. But as one chemical is phased out, several more are developed and added to the toxic soup. A new family of chemicals called poly-brominated diphenyl ethers (PBDEs) are of particular concern. PBDEs are used as flame-retardants on everything from carpets to computers. Their presence has been detected in orcas, long-finned pilot whales and deep-diving sperm whales, indicating that they are accumulating down in the ocean depths. Little is known about the impact of these chemicals on humans. There are three PBDE formulations. Two, which are known to have similar toxic properties to PCBs, have been withdrawn from the market in Europe and North America although they are still produced in Asia. More worryingly, production of the third form is greatly increasing worldwide on the basis of early research, which demonstrated that it is much safer to use than the other two formulations. However, this evidence is being revised with new findings indicating that it is crossing into food webs. Many scientists are predicting that PBDEs will surpass PCBs as the number one contaminant in wildlife in the next ten to 20 years.

THE IMPACT OF CONTAMINANTS on whales and dolphins extends to the people who eat them. Inuit populations in the Arctic are especially at risk as their once pristine polar home is now a hotspot for pollution. A suite of chemical compounds produced and deployed in warm and temperate latitudes travels in the atmosphere until it reaches the Arctic and condenses in the cold temperatures. The fish, seals and cetaceans on which Inuit societies rely absorb these pollutants from the environment. As a result the Inuit, who have resisted many of the trappings of modern life, are among the most contaminated people on the planet. A Canadian study found that among indigenous communities in Greenland, where beluga and narwhal mattak – the skin and blubber – make up a significant part of the diet, 95% of women exceed the Canadian government's recommended limits for PCB contamination. Much of this burden is transferred to newborn babies, with potentially tragic consequences.

Those who eat cetacean products containing heavy metals face even greater health problems. Metals, principally mercury, accumulate in the muscles, liver, kidneys and other organs of whales and dolphins. Mercury is produced by natural processes such as the weathering of rocks, and has long had its place in the environment, but in recent times industrial plants have increased the amount in the atmosphere three-fold. Coal-burning power works and waste incinerators are the main culprits but a significant amount also leaches into the environment from discarded manufactured goods such as thermometers, dental fillings and fluorescent lights.

Mercury is highly toxic and extremely persistent. When deposited in the ocean, some is converted into a substance called methylmercury by the action of bacteria. Methylmercury is even more toxic than mercury and accumulates more rapidly in animals' bodies. As levels found in cetaceans rise the issue is gaining importance in whale-eating nations. Methylmercury from contaminated meat can cause irreversible neurological damage in humans and it crosses the placental barrier easily so unborn children are especially at risk. Japan, Norway, Iceland and the Faroe Islands have all circulated health warnings regarding the consumption of contaminated products. The long-finned pilot whale hunted by the Faroe Islanders contains an alarming cocktail of toxins. Its meat is laced with both mercury and another heavy metal, cadmium. This may reflect the whale's choice of prey – their favoured squid is known as a cadmium accumulator – as well as a particular inability to flush toxins from their bodies. Furthermore, pilot whale blubber is loaded with PCBs. Studies have revealed worryingly high mercury levels in new mothers, while the average concentration of PCBs in the breast milk of Faroe Island women is ten times that found in Swedish mothers.

The Faroese advice recognises the threat to all consumers, but Japan, Norway and Iceland direct their warnings only to pregnant and breastfeeding women. However, mercury burdens accrue over a lifetime so if a woman renounces whale meat only when she conceives it may too late to save her baby from its effects. In Japan, the world's top consumer of cetacean products, official guidelines fall far short of being truly effective. Between 2002 and 2005 Japanese researchers travelled the length and breadth of the country, buying and testing samples. They found that every single slice of whale and dolphin meat contained levels of mercury that exceeded the legal limit, with the most contaminated product carrying 87 times the maximum dosage. According to government guidelines a person weighing 60 kg (132 lb) could consume only 4 g of this meat in a week if they were to stay inside the recommended limits. Moreover, toothed whale and dolphin products are often mislabelled as 'minke whale', leading consumers to believe that they are buying less contaminated baleen whales from Japan's Antarctic research programme.

The dangers of mercury are well established in Japan. In the 1950s and 1960s, 3000 adults in the region around Minamata Bay suffered brain damage and other disorders of the central nervous system, while hundreds of children were born with severe deformities. For over 30 years raw mercury compounds had been poured into the bay. The victims were poisoned by contaminated fish and contracted what has become known as Minamata disease. In light of this tragedy it is especially surprising that more stringent controls are not in place.

THE TWIN PRESSURES of climate change and marine pollution do not act in isolation but can impact on each other. Warmer seas provide perfect conditions for the transmission of infectious diseases to which cetaceans, with immune systems compromised by chemical pollution, will more readily succumb. Animals with weakened constitutions are also less likely to survive the devastating storms predicted by many climate change experts.

In addition to essential initiatives to reduce emissions of greenhouse gases, some conservation groups have suggested that the best way to protect cetaceans and other marine mammals would be to designate protected areas that operate as no-take zones for both mammals and their prey. But as weather systems are constantly shifting, the ideal location for such sanctuaries will move over time, so the boundaries would need to be regularly re-evaluated and redefined. This would represent a radical departure from current modes of practice, requiring new systems of international cooperation and great commitment to be truly effective.

Chemicals need tackling at source. There are too many in the world to allow full research on the potential and actual effects of all of them, so the best way forward would be to prioritise. Criteria for assessment should include the level of production and release into the environment, known toxicity and potential for bioaccumulation. The production of novel but hazardous compounds like PBDEs should be assessed as a matter of urgency. Comprehensive research programmes to determine levels of contamination and consumption should be instituted in all the countries where cetaceans are eaten. The sale of contaminated products needs to be tightly monitored and controlled. In a curious twist to the whaling saga, it may be the ailing health of many cetacean populations, rather than any number of arguments about species abundance and the ethics of hunting, that leads to whales and dolphins being taken off the menu.

Close encounters

On captivity, collaboration and intelligence

Ever since humans began venturing out to sea they have had close encounters with whales and dolphins. At one extreme, contact is made when we seize cetaceans from the wild and compel them to live in captivity. The majority of captives are held to entertain the public, but others are kept by research facilities or pressed into military service. In other circumstances, the contact is initiated by the animal and is entirely voluntary; some dolphins are famously friendly and actively seek out human company, while in exceptional cases cetaceans have been known to rescue swimmers in distress or help fishermen to collect the day's catch. These interactions reinforce the idea that cetaceans are special and far more intelligent than most other animals.

In the summer of 1861 thousands of New Yorkers stood patiently in line, waiting to catch a glimpse of an animal they had never seen before. P.T. Barnum, the great American showman and circus pioneer, had caught two beluga whales in Canada's St

Lawrence River and transported them to a brick-and-cement tank in the basement of his Manhattan museum. Kept in fresh water and breathing stagnant air, the luckless whales perished within days, but not before they had become the talk of the town. A reporter for the *New York Tribune* captured the excitement inspired by the exhibition:

> "A real live whale is as great a curiosity as a live lord or prince, being much more difficult to catch, and far more wonderful in its appearance and habits ... Here is a real 'sensation'. We do not believe the enterprise of Mr Barnum will stop at white whales. It will embrace sperm whales and mermaids, and all strange things that swim or fly or crawl, until the Museum will become one vast microcosm of the animal creation. A quarter seems positively contemptible weighed against such a treat."

Barnum responded to the whales' untimely demise by sending off to Canada for some more. Thus the industry in captive whales and dolphins was born. Today, as the undisputed stars of marine parks and aquaria, these charismatic creatures continue to attract large crowds. Since Barnum's day at least 25 species, including Pacific white-sided dolphins, killer whales, false killer whales and Irrawaddy dolphins, have been taken into captivity. But the cetacean most commonly held in marine parks, and arguably the most familiar of its kind, is the bottlenose dolphin.

In the late 1930s Marine Studios, the first dedicated oceanarium, opened in Florida. It was here that it became apparent how easy bottlenose dolphins are to train. Their popularity soared and soon a booming trade was operating out of Florida, with dolphins being exported to the rest of the USA and to Europe. During the 1950s, 1960s and 1970s, public enthusiasm steadily increased and more and more facilities were opened. But towards the end of this period, as attitudes to nature changed and the international campaign against whaling gathered momentum, ethical arguments against keeping cetaceans in captivity also began to flourish. The campaign against captivity is now being waged with unprecedented energy. The public display industry maintains that the exhibition of cetaceans not only entertains people but also serves a valuable role in education, research and conservation, while the animals enjoy a comfortable existence. But animal protection groups and many scientists refute these justifications. They argue that whales and dolphins are fundamentally unsuited to a life of captivity, and that to confine them is immoral and cruel.

Of all the cetaceans in captivity the species that pulls the biggest crowds and excites the most controversy is the orca. The orca's immense popularity is a consequence of its striking appearance, its trainability and its sheer size; males average more than 7 m (23 ft) in length; females are a little shorter. In January 2006, 45 orcas were being held by 13 marine parks in six countries. SeaWorld maintains 21 of these animals. This chain of marine parks, owned by the brewing giant Anheuser Busch, dominates the industry in the USA. Collectively, the SeaWorld parks receive more than 10 million visitors a year. An estimated 70% of their income derives from customers attracted to the orca shows.

The first orca held in captivity was a female caught in Californian waters in 1961. She was surrounded by boats, trapped with nets, and taken to 'Marineland of the Pacific' near Los Angeles. She swam around her tank at high speed, repeatedly ramming the sides, and died just a day later. The orca collectors were not deterred. After a number of subsequent mishaps they discovered effective ways to sequester the animals. They surrounded them with purse-seine nets or waited until a pod swam into a harbour or shallow inlet and quickly blocked the exit. They could then select the individuals they wanted at leisure. The orcas' staunch social bonds made the collectors' task easier because the animals tended to huddle in a group rather than flee in different directions.

From 1964 at least 56 orcas were taken from the North Pacific off the coasts of Washington State and British Columbia. Of these one escaped, 53 have died, and two – Corky and Lolita – are still alive. In 1976 the captures were outlawed in response to growing public concern at their frequency and the number of animal deaths. Demand for orcas had not abated, however, so American collectors moved their operations to Iceland whose government welcomed them with open arms. Orcas had a bad reputation amongst Icelandic fishermen who perceived them as competitors for valuable herring stocks. Selling orcas to the Americans seemed an ideal opportunity to generate income while gratifying the powerful fishing lobby. Between 1976 and 1989, at

An orca is put through its paces in an American marine park. Note the drooping dorsal fin.

least 55 individuals were taken into captivity. Eventually campaigning by conservation groups and international pressure brought the business to a close there as well.

Orcas became harder to acquire as they gained protection in a growing number of countries. Their commercial value rose accordingly and an orca is now worth in excess of US$1 million. Japanese aquaria take animals from their own waters but to date, none have been sold overseas. Russia has shown interest in supplying the international market but so far its plans have not met with success. Its intentions are of great concern to conservation groups because little is known about the size and health of Russian orca populations. In the USA there are restrictions on permits for importing wild-caught orcas from abroad. Animal welfare groups believe that this has motivated SeaWorld and other parks to engage in highly dubious transactions that amount to 'orca laundering'. The parks have allegedly arranged for overseas facilities to capture wild animals and hold them for several years, after which time they can be legally imported to the USA as 'already captive' animals, or 'breeding loans'.

Dolphins are captured using a number of techniques. Collectors may drive them into shallow waters, or encircle them with purse-seine nets in open water. Bow-riding species such as Pacific white-sided dolphins can be collared with specially designed lassoes. A six-fold spike in mortality risk, compared to natural levels, has been reported during and immediately after capture. There have been no wild captures of dolphins in the USA since 1993 but the industry is thriving in the Caribbean, Asia and the South Pacific.

The other species held in significant numbers is Barnum's favourite, the beluga whale. Until 1994, when a local moratorium on their capture was established, belugas were caught in Canada by 'cold water cowboys' who corralled them into the shallows using speedboats, roped them, leapt onto their backs rodeo-style and wrestled them into submission. They are now caught and exported worldwide from Russia.

Once in captivity a cetacean's fate is determined by geography and luck. There are no international minimum standards in place and while some countries enforce fairly stringent regulations, others do not. The most fortunate captives are kept in large, deep, coastal enclosures filled naturally with seawater, and given a healthy and varied diet. Of the completely artificial facilities, those in North America and Europe tend to be relatively well-funded and designed, although the animals' needs are always balanced with the visiting public's desire to see them up close. In many other nations, where financial constraints and space limitations are coupled with a lack of knowledge, cetaceans are often consigned to live in cramped, featureless concrete tanks.

Animal welfare campaigners contend that it is impossible to satisfy the physical, social and mental needs of such large, gregarious and intelligent animals in a captive situation. The species commonly held by marine parks would naturally spend their days ranging over large distances, foraging and hunting for food, avoiding predators, diving, resting, playing, and maintaining strong family bonds and complex social networks. But in captivity their natural behaviours atrophy. Individuals may live alone, or cohabit with animals from other pods, other oceans or even other species – a critical welfare issue for social beings. Their tanks may be filled with chemically treated water filtered by pumps that create a constant drone. They are forced to adapt to a diet of frozen fish, topped up by regular vitamin and mineral pills. In even high-quality facilities the requirements of maintenance and hygiene often dictate smooth, concrete surfaces that cannot provide the visual and acoustic stimulation of the multi-textured and ever-changing natural environment.

The public display industry maintains that a captive animal's quality of life is not compromised, but is in fact enhanced. The animals lose their freedom and natural companions, but in return are protected from the myriad pitfalls and hardships of life in the wild. They never go hungry and they never encounter predators, parasites, natural disasters, commercial fishing nets, ships or chemical pollution. Instead they receive an ample and reliable supply of food, and the highest possible standard of medical care. But animal welfare groups dismiss such claims as nonsense. They argue that cetaceans are superbly adapted to face the natural challenges of life in the wild and that hazards caused by human activity are best dealt with in other ways. In contrast, captives suffer unceasing physical and mental stress. This can manifest in aggression between themselves and towards humans, lower life expectancy and higher infant mortality.

A particularly striking symptom of captivity is exhibited by mature male orcas, whose lofty, 1.8 m (6 ft) long dorsal fins gradually droop to one side and eventually collapse. This phenomenon is almost universal in captive animals but is seldom observed in the wild. There is no scientific consensus as to the cause, but it is thought that gravity may exert a lop-sided pull on whales that rarely dive and have to swim in circles. Moreover, by spending most of the day at the water's surface they are exposed to excessive sunlight, which may alter the structure of the fin's collagen.

Despite the denials of marine parks, there is no doubt that cetaceans experiencing long-term, unalleviated stress can become aggressive. Violent outbursts are more likely to occur when incompatible animals are housed together. Dominant dolphins have been observed intimidating subordinates with jaw claps, biting, ramming and tail slaps. This behaviour is also observed in the wild, but in captivity the subordinate animal cannot get away. The imprudence of ignoring the fundamental role of hierarchy in animal societies was highlighted in 1989 when Kandu, a dominant young female orca, rammed into her pool mate, Corky, in front of a full stadium. Although Corky survived the assault,

Kandu ruptured an artery in her own jaw. She spouted blood as the shocked spectators were ushered out, and died 45 minutes later. Attacks on trainers can also be a problem. Throughout the 1980s a number of park personnel sustained permanent injuries during a particularly bad run of incidents. Then in 1991 tragedy occurred when a young trainer, Keltie Byrne, slipped and fell into the orca pool at Sealand of the Pacific in British Columbia. She was held underwater by three orcas and drowned.

The survival rates of whales and dolphins held in captivity provoke fierce debate. Marine parks insist that their charges live as long as wild animals, but definitive statistics are thin on the ground. The parks, notoriously reluctant to release details of deaths to outsiders, veil their records in secrecy. Furthermore, the life histories of wild populations are not always perfectly understood – marine parks tend to adopt lower estimates of wild lifespans while advocacy groups sometimes cite maximum longevity as an average.

The most comprehensive data available applies to orcas, which unarguably live longer in the wild. Of the 135 individuals taken into captivity since 1961, 117 (87%) are now dead. The annual mortality rate of captive orcas is 6-7%, three times that of wild animals. The mortality of bottlenose dolphins in captivity and in the wild is thought to be roughly equal. For other species insufficient knowledge of life history parameters in the wild proscribes legitimate comparisons.

EVERY YEAR MILLIONS OF PEOPLE experience the thrill of seeing captive cetaceans race around their tanks in perfect synchrony, toss balls, swim through hoops, 'kiss' their trainers and execute impressive acrobatic stunts. The animals are usually trained using a method called 'operant conditioning' in which food rewards are used as positive reinforcement. Marine parks believe that their animals are stimulated and exercised by training and performing. Routines, they claim, are adequate substitutes for the natural exertions of hunting. They also assure doubters that the animals' participation is entirely voluntary, and that their antics do more than simply entertain the visiting public.

In the USA marine parks are required to provide education and conservation programmes by federal law. Although some parks promote themselves as centres of excellence in these fields, the true value of their programmes is repeatedly called into question by animal welfare and conservation organisations. They condemn the parks for cynically using buzzwords to gain the trust and approval of an unsuspecting public. The parks, they say, are maintaining a false veneer of respectability and paying only lip service to their requirements. Their real aim is to keep the money rolling in.

Industry rhetoric maintains that the shows foster respect and understanding. In recent years the performances have been refocused to incorporate information about the animals' natural lives. The parks claim that visitors who lack the opportunity to witness dolphins cavorting in the wild will be inspired by experiencing them in the flesh. They are likely to develop an enhanced appreciation of wildlife and a more committed conservation ethic. Animal welfare campaigners retort that a performing whale or dolphin is a grotesque parody of its wild counterpart. The performers' apparent gaiety desensitises spectators to the cruel reality of removing animals from their natural habitat. The calibre of educational material is highly questionable, and very little information is retained as visitors get swept up in the excitement of the show.

There have been few studies carried out to furnish the debate with hard evidence. There is no doubt that attitudes towards whales and dolphins have transformed in the last 50 years. Many deep-rooted misconceptions have been banished and support for their conservation has burgeoned. Once widely perceived as blood-thirsty, ferocious predators, orcas are now celebrated and adored. Commercial aquaria are keen to take some of the credit as catalysts for change, and they may indeed be entitled to some. The sea change in perceptions of 'killer whales' coincided with their first appearances in captivity, supporting the argument that captive individuals can act as ambassadors for their species. The transformation in attitudes towards dolphins can be attributed to a number of cultural phenomena: their exposure at marine parks; the popular TV series *Flipper*; and the work of Jacques Cousteau and other film-making pioneers who beamed images of the underwater world into people's homes for the first time.

But since much of that work has been done, do marine parks still play a valid role in shaping attitudes? Modern thinking highlights the importance of understanding and conserving wildlife as nature intended, and the practice of compromising animals' lives for our entertainment looks increasingly anachronistic. Additionally, some marine parks may be deliberately misleading the public. The gulf between image and reality is epitomised by what orca expert Erich Hoyt has called the 'Shamu lie'. Shamu is a fabricated orca – a potent combination of myth and marketing. In the 1970s SeaWorld decided to use the same few names for all its performing orcas. The names are passed from animal to animal and 'Shamu' has become the best known. While Shamu merchandise flies off the shelves, the heritability of the name conveniently masks the deaths of individual animals. As a spokesman said, following the death of one of the orcas at SeaWorld's Texas park in 1991, "Shamu has not died today. One of the whales who plays that role we lost this morning, yes. But Shamu lives on."

Another alleged benefit of keeping cetaceans in captivity is that they can be used for vital scientific research. Not all laboratory animals are kept in marine parks as a number of dedicated research facilities also exist. Techniques for studying wild animals are more advanced than ever before, but there is some information that can only be gleaned from captives. Researchers can train them to participate in tests, observe them around the clock, and monitor bodily fluids or behavioural reactions at regular intervals. For these reasons, they are still a significant source of data for studies of comparative psychology, physiology, reproduction, acoustics, hearing, brain function and veterinary medicine.

Although many scientists believe that much research has been useful, the value of some studies has been questioned. Some detractors believe that the research agendas of marine parks are shaped by the necessity of keeping captives alive, rather than any grand schemes to enhance scientific knowledge. They argue that most information on health and behaviour obtained from captives cannot be applied to wild animals whose lives are so different. Some diseases infect both populations, particularly bacterial pneumonia, but improved veterinary knowledge has been of little benefit during the mass mortality events, or 'die offs', that have ravaged some wild stocks in recent years. Furthermore, information on visual, acoustic and echolocation systems derived from animals in spartan tanks, while undoubtedly interesting, might not be meaningful when extrapolated to the noisy, turbulent, murky waters in which wild whales and dolphins live.

Captive breeding is another controversial issue. In the USA and Canada breeding programmes have been prioritised as the capture and import of wild animals has become restricted, and the creation of an 'environmentally sound' image has gained importance. SeaWorld has invested heavily in its captive breeding programme and its success, although patchy, is unrivalled. The robust bottlenose dolphin has proved relatively easy to breed but orcas are more of a challenge – of 69 known pregnancies since 1968 only 29 (42%) of the calves survived. Beluga whales are sometimes bred successfully; at least eight individuals born in captivity survived the critical first few months.

Conservation groups are infuriated by marine parks that promote themselves as conservation concerns, propagating and maintaining a bank of animals as security against extinction in the wild. The aim of genuine captive breeding programmes is to replenish depleted wild populations, but to date marine parks have shown little interest in releasing captives. Their limited breeding success benefits wild populations only insofar as it reduces the need to obtain fresh stocks from the ocean. Marine parks also try to bolster their green credentials by claiming that their experience could help rescue highly endangered animals like China's river dolphin, the baiji. But conservationists remain sceptical as to the broader utility of their expertise. The baiji is a completely different animal whose anatomy, physiology, social structure and behaviour differ markedly to any captive species.

The viability of release programmes is extremely contentious. Many animal protection advocates insist that success can be achieved if operations are immaculately planned and closely monitored. Marine parks, whose captives are the lifeblood of their enterprises, counter that it is inhumane to liberate animals that may have lost the ability to hunt, socialise and deal with the diverse challenges of life in the wild. These arguments somewhat undermine their own captive breeding assertions. There have been some successful releases of bottlenose dolphins, but only a single attempt has been made with an orca. His name was Keiko.

Keiko was the star of Warner Brothers Studios' phenomenally successful film, *Free Willy*. He was caught in Iceland in 1979 at a young age. After spending some time in dolphinaria in Iceland and Canada he was sold to a facility in Mexico, where he lived in a small tank with only a sea lion for company. His story took an unexpected twist when he was plucked from obscurity to play Willy, a morose orca living in a seedy marine park who is helped to freedom by his human friend Jesse. After filming, Keiko languished in his tank until media reports revealed his living conditions and failing health, and just how closely life can imitate art. A worldwide campaign to secure the whale's release was launched.

Thanks to the collaborative efforts of animal protection groups, Warner Brothers Studios, a private benefactor and a range of other sponsors, Keiko was repatriated to Iceland in 1998. He was housed in a specially constructed sea pen, weaned off frozen fish, taught how to catch live prey, taken on supervised forays into the open ocean, and fitted with a radio and satellite-tracking device on his dorsal fin. Keiko started interacting with local wild orcas and in 2002 set off on a 1500 km (900 mile) journey across the Atlantic. He arrived in a Norwegian fjord five weeks later, in good health but alone, having failed to integrate into a wild pod. Apparently seeking human company, Keiko stayed in the fjord and allowed ecstatic children to ride on his back. In an attempt to break his dependency he was then moved to an isolated inlet where he lived until his sudden death, probably from pneumonia, in 2003. The operation cost millions of dollars and attracted considerable criticism from the outset. Many felt the money might have been better spent elsewhere, although without Keiko the funds would not have been raised in the first place.

Keiko enjoyed only a few years of liberty but the exercise invigorated campaigners and greatly raised the profile of captive orcas.

The controversy surrounding captive cetaceans has spiralled in many countries over the last 20 years. As the public grew disenchanted during the 1990s the number of marine parks holding captive cetaceans in Australia, New Zealand, some parts of Europe and North America declined. The list of countries that ban the import, export or display of live cetaceans is growing. This downsizing has, however, been matched by an increase in the number of facilities in other parts of the world, including Asia, the Caribbean and South America. In some of these countries there is little in the way of animal rights activism and meagre regulation.

A worrying trend, as far as campaigners are concerned, is the proliferation of opportunities to touch, feed and swim with dolphins. Marine parks are raising their game by establishing 'swim with the dolphins' programmes and 'petting pools'. Campaigners fear that this dramatic growth, combined with a lack of legislation, is a recipe for disaster. Although a close encounter with a

A hands-on encounter with bottlenose dolphins in the Bahamas.

dolphin is an undeniably moving and exciting experience, insufficient attention is paid to the potential consequences of such intimacy. Petting pools are often inadequately supervised, with hundreds of people crowding round the animals. The dolphins may grow obese from overfeeding, they may be fed inappropriate foods or ingest dangerous foreign objects, and there is no accounting for the hygiene of fish they receive from the hands of visitors. The public are also at risk — dolphins have been known to bite, head butt and squash hands against tank walls. Marine parks portray dolphins as gentle and friendly and many visitors, especially those who hold their young children over the pool, forget that these are not only wild animals, but predators. With their permanent smiles it is hard to imagine that the dolphins may be experiencing severe stress. There are similar concerns about facilities in which the public swim with dolphins. Dolphins often respond to human swimmers by behaving in a submissive manner. This could indicate that the animal is stressed and may encourage other group members to exert their dominance.

Most of the discourse on the rights and wrongs of keeping captive cetaceans takes place in a Western context. In many other countries the cultural perspective on animal rights is quite different. It is just possible that the expansion of marine parks in these countries will kindle a change in public attitudes to cetaceans, as happened in Europe and North America. But if the animals are displayed inappropriately their exhibition may not cultivate thoughtful appreciation, and the price paid by captive individuals and the wild populations from which they were removed may be too high.

A key question is whether people will care about animals if they cannot actually see them. California's Monterey Bay aquarium is a much lauded and very popular enterprise. In place of live cetaceans it features beautiful life-size models and a camera beaming in underwater action from the bay. Modern facilities can also make use of animatronics, 3D and large-screen cinema technology, virtual reality simulations and interactive museum-style displays. Undeniably, such exhibits do not trigger the same emotional response as living, breathing animals, but they can inspire and inform.

SOME CAPTIVE DOLPHINS are used to provide therapy. This novel form of healing is growing in popularity. It is also extremely controversial. Proponents have claimed miraculous benefits for patients suffering from a range of conditions including cerebral palsy, Down's syndrome, autism, severe depression and learning difficulties. Dissenters argue that the practice is untested, exploitative, risky for the clients and unkind to the animals. There is an abundance of anecdotal evidence testifying to the healing power of dolphins, but a paucity of objective data to back it up. It has been suggested that the sounds the dolphins make may relax patients, reduce stress and boost the recovery process, or that the emotional impact of interacting with animals brings wider health benefits. Such possibilities support the theory of biophilia, first put forward by the sociobiologist Edward O. Wilson, that human health and emotions are strongly influenced by the natural environment. Intuitively it makes sense that exposure to natural scenery and beguiling animals promotes happiness.

But opponents of dolphin therapy feel that it is an inappropriate practice. They believe that the risk of aggression and disease transmission jeopardises the welfare of both dolphins and patients. The desperate parents of sick children are particularly vulnerable to abuse by unscrupulous practitioners offering an unproven but extremely expensive cure. It is not known how long the positive effects persist, and whether similar results can be obtained by using domestic animals such as puppies and kittens. If they can, then there is indeed little justification for creating a rather dubious interaction with 'nature' through the confinement of wild animals.

AMONG THE DELUGE OF MEDIA ARTICLES published in the wake of Hurricane Katrina, which devastated New Orleans in 2005, were a number that warned of bizarre dangers lurking in the Gulf of Mexico. The articles alleged that armed dolphins, trained by the US Navy to identify and perhaps shoot enemy swimmers with toxic dart guns, had been swept out to sea when the hurricane destroyed their coastal compound. The story was quickly dismissed as a hoax, but like many conspiracy theories it had its origins in fact.

Over the years the US Navy has conscripted a number of cetaceans. Its Marine Mammal Program was launched in the 1960s, during the cold war, with the acquisition of a Pacific white-sided dolphin. Navy scientists wanted to understand the dolphin's hydrodynamic capabilities in order to improve the performance of torpedoes. The technology of the day failed to identify the dolphin's special qualities, but the researchers took note of its intelligence, trainability and exceptional diving skills. The idea that dolphins could contribute to a modern military was born.

The Navy researchers soon realised that echolocation, the most advanced sonar known to science, made dolphins uniquely effective at locating objects under water. Bottlenose dolphins were the first species to be trained. Beluga whales, which can operate in much colder waters and at greater depths than dolphins, were later added to the list of recruits, as were sea lions. The Navy now runs five marine mammal teams, each dedicated to a specific type of mission. Some animals have been taught to identify sea mines, while others deliver equipment to divers, or find and retrieve lost objects. Marine mammals also work as sentries, protecting vessels, piers and harbours from acts of sabotage by alerting their handlers to the presence of unauthorised swimmers.

Dolphins first saw active service in Vietnam in 1971. Their role was to warn of enemy divers approaching ammunition piers and to tag them with a marker. Rumours circulated of a 'swimmer nullification program' in which assassin dolphins were trained to kill, but the Navy has consistently and strenuously denied that any

A US Navy dolphin tags an imitation sea mine during training exercises.

such initiative ever existed. Despite their insistence, and the Marine Mammal Program's eventual declassification in the 1990s, the scheme has been dogged by controversy since its inception. While some allegations seem plausible, others stretch the limits of credibility. Claims have even been made that the Soviet military's parallel programme involved training dolphins to be covertly airdropped into foreign waters with the aid of parachutes.

It is thought that the Russian military abandoned its marine mammal programme in the 1990s. The US Navy's operation has been reduced but still operates from its base in San Diego. Dolphins patrolled harbours in Bahrain during the Iran-Iraq war in 1986/87, and were dispatched to the Iraqi port of Umm Qasr in 2003 to help clear it of mines. Unsurprisingly, the majority of animal welfare groups maintain that it is completely unacceptable to exploit cetaceans in this way.

NOT ALL THE RELATIONSHIPS between people and cetaceans are enforced; in some cases they are entirely voluntary. There are countless stories of 'friendly' dolphins seeking human company or heroically rescuing stricken swimmers. Whales – the mythically colossal inhabitants of the deep ocean – are treated with suspicion by the folklore of many cultures, but dolphins are almost always portrayed as sweet-tempered, trusting animals blessed with an almost human-like intelligence and capacity for compassion.

Herodotus was the first to pen a story about a dolphin lifeguard in the fifth century BC. The tale features Arion, the finest lyre-player of his day. Arion's musical performances had made him extremely rich. Following a lucrative tour of Italy he hired a crew to sail him back to his native Greece. On the way the treacherous sailors plotted to kill him and steal his fortune but Arion bargained with them and was allowed to perform one last number before being cast overboard. Fortunately the beauty of his voice enchanted a passing dolphin, which rescued him in the swell and carried him and his lyre to safety.

More recently, in 2004, a pod of bottlenose dolphins came to the rescue when a great white shark approached some swimmers off the coast of New Zealand. The dolphins herded the group together and turned tight circles around them, slapping the water with their tails, until the shark lost interest. There is no clear reason as to why dolphins would put themselves out in this way. Scientists are often sceptical. They maintain that the animals' intentions and behaviour cannot be easily interpreted and point out that dolphins sometimes cause human swimmers harm. But dolphins frequently cooperate to assist their own kind in times of difficulty, and it seems that on occasion they are willing to extend this protection to a completely different species.

There are countless stories of lone dolphins deliberately courting human company. This phenomenon may occur because an animal has separated from its own group and its natural sociality finds a different focus. A well-documented case is that of Pelorus Jack. A solitary Risso's dolphin, Pelorus Jack escorted ferry steamers through New Zealand's French Pass, a perilous channel cluttered with rocks and swept by strong currents. He became a regular fixture in the Pass from 1888 and saved countless vessels from the risk of shipwreck. In 1904 he became the first dolphin to be granted legal protection after a drunken passenger tried to shoot him. Pelorus Jack was last seen alive in 1912 but is remembered fondly to this day.

Some cetaceans collaborate with humans to hunt. In Mauritania fishermen summon dolphins to help them catch mullet. When the migrating fish appear close to shore the men slap the surface of the water with sticks. Attracted by the commotion the dolphins leap into action and block the mullets' escape along the seaward edge. The dolphins feast on the cornered fish while the fishermen harvest the bounty with nets. In the town of Laguna, Brazil, a similar partnership exists – when the dolphins roll over on the water's surface the men take it as a signal to cast their nets. But possibly the most extraordinary tale of all comes from the small town of Eden on Australia's east coast. From the 1860s until 1930 men and orcas cooperated to hunt humpback whales. The orcas waylaid a whale in open sea and harried and herded it into an enclosed bay. They then alerted the whalers by noisily thumping the water with their tail flukes. At dawn the men would set out, following the orcas' lead, and slaughter the great whale. But instead of towing the carcass back to shore, the fishermen anchored it in the shallows and left it to float for a day. They were honouring an understanding with the orcas and allowing them to eat their share, usually consisting of the tongue and surrounding jawline. The next day the men collected what was left.

WHEN HUMANS ENCOUNTER CETACEANS, whether they are training them to perform for the public or catching fish with them, they contemplate the intelligence of these remarkable animals. Dolphins, in particular, are frequently admired as preternaturally clever animals – the marine equivalent of the great apes. But just how smart are they? Before answering that question it is necessary to raise the issue of what exactly intelligence is.

Although the meaning of the word is broadly understood by everyone, its exact definition is open to interpretation. Intelligence is an entity that is difficult to pin down, measure and compare within humans. It is considerably harder to assess it in other species.

Little is known of the intelligence of great whales because it is impossible to study them in captivity. Much more work has been done with dolphins. One of the early pioneers in the field was an American scientist, John Lilly. In the 1950s Lilly became fascinated by the mind hidden within the human brain. In his quest to reveal its workings he began studying an animal with a brain of roughly equal size – the bottlenose dolphin. After a number of false starts, in which anaesthetised dolphins stopped breathing and died, Lilly embarked on two parallel lines of inquiry. One was an investigation into the possibility of human-dolphin communication, the other was an exploration of the outer reaches of human consciousness. In the late 1960s he began experimenting with mind-altering drugs, and found himself at the vanguard of the emerging, California-based counterculture of New Age scientists, mystics and radicals. But in his search for a higher truth, Lilly lost his way.

Lilly believed that dolphins communicated with a sophisti-cated language. He claimed to have taught dolphins to mimic human speech, but his experiments have never been successfully replicated. He also attributed dolphins with sage-like ethical qualities and mental capacities rivalling or surpassing that of humans. He wrote of what people could learn from dolphins, once the communication problem had been solved. Some saw Lilly as a brilliant visionary, but many in the scientific community thought he was deluded. Nonetheless, his depiction of dolphins as gifted beings with vibrant emotional lives governed by a liberal moral code resonated with the public. Lilly published numerous books that sold millions of copies worldwide and his ideas spread. The superior intelligence of dolphins was frequently taken as fact, and people spoke of a language called delphinese as if it existed. Although much of Lilly's research has been discredited, the image of the dolphin he helped to construct persists.

NOWADAYS RESEARCHERS USE A NUMBER of approaches to delve into cetacean intelligence. Some look at anatomy. While no single feature provides a straightforward indication of high intelligence, brain size and structure are obvious places to start looking for clues. Whales and dolphins have large brains, but then they also have large bodies. Large animals tend to have bigger brains than small animals, irrespective of acumen, so absolute brain size is too crude a measure to be meaningful. However, the size of the brain relative to the size of the body has long been perceived as informative of intelligence. Various measures have been devised, the most popular of which is the Encephalization Quotient (EQ). The EQ is an index that compares an animal's actual brain mass to the mass that would be predicted given the animal's size.

Some cetaceans boast high EQs but not all. The sperm whale's brain might be the largest on Earth, but its 8 kg (18 lb) mass is relatively insignificant when appraised in the context of its 37,000 kg (81,000 lb) body. Bottlenose dolphins, Pacific white-sided dolphins and short-beaked common dolphins all have high EQ's, but they cannot compete with humans whose scores are approximately double. However, the tallies for all cetaceans improve considerably if allowances are made for their disproportionately large bodies and plentiful, heavy blubber. Indeed, the enormous body masses of sperm whales and mysticetes may render brain-to-body ratios as largely irrelevant tools in the analysis of their intelligence.

The structure and complexity of an animal's brain may also reveal something about its intelligence. In cetaceans the cerebrum – the largest part of the brain and the seat of conscious thought and sense interpretation – is well developed. The top layer, the neocortex, is a smooth surface in many mammals but has deep grooves and wrinkles in humans, primates and cetaceans. Long thought to be an indication of exceptional intelligence, this elaborate folding may simply act to increase the brain's surface area. Ultimately, anatomy can give a rough idea of intelligence, but only a vague indication of an animal's complexity of thought. A more fruitful approach is to look at behaviour.

Some behaviours are classic indicators of intelligence. Species that interact in complex ways and exhibit novel responses to new situations – as do most cetaceans – are likely to be more intelligent than those whose communication is simpler and more rigid. The ability to learn is another positive sign. A study of a performing rough-toothed dolphin called Malia, carried out at Sea Life Park in Hawaii in the mid 1960s, illuminates her species' capacity for inventiveness. Malia was trained, by operant conditioning, to perform new stunts as part of her act. It took just a few days for her to discern that only novel moves would be rewarded. She began performing spectacular exploits, skidding along the tank floor and executing aerial acrobatics that had never been seen at the park before. The experiment was successfully repeated with another dolphin, Hou. The results do not demonstrate a unique capacity for creativity because horses and even pigeons can also be trained for novelty, but there is no doubt that the dolphins grasped the concept with impressive speed. In similar tests carried out on human volunteers, the subjects took a comparable amount of time to catch on. Both the humans and dolphins experienced a period of frustration when they could not work out what was required. Once they realised, the humans expressed feelings of relief, while the dolphins zoomed around their tank in great excitement.

Some cetaceans also exhibit 'cultural transmission' where animals develop new behaviours and pass them onto their cohorts by social learning. Female bottlenose dolphins off the west coast of Australia have acquired an innovative technique to protect themselves from the spines and stingers of sea creatures while foraging. They break off marine sponges and place them over their beaks. The behaviour seems to pass almost exclusively from mothers to daughters; male dolphins generally do not follow suit for reasons unknown. In Patagonia young orcas appear to be taught, by their mothers or other females, to beach themselves in order to catch sea lion and elephant seal pups on the sand. This is a high-risk exercise since the whale needs to strand itself at the right speed and angle to ensure the breaking waves will carry it back out to deeper water. Adults have been observed making sham rushes at the beach and then retreating to the side while the novices try to copy them. The young whales often botch their first attempts and it may take numerous rehearsals to get it right.

Another much-cited sign of intelligence is the cetacean propensity for play. Almost all young mammals play as a means of developing the skills they will need to survive. But some whales and dolphins seem to take particular delight in their antics. Dusky dolphins sneak up under floating sea birds and pull their legs, and several species balance pieces of seaweed, stones or fish parts on their snouts and flippers. Orcas have been observed tossing stingrays to each other like Frisbees although rather than playing they may actually be stunning the rays to disable their stings before eating them.

In humans, intelligence is intimately connected with the use of language. The same could be true of communication in cetaceans. Most work has been done with dolphins, which can be observed in laboratory conditions. Dolphins emit clicks for echolocation and communicate with whistles and 'burst pulse sounds', which they may use to indicate their emotional state. It is not known exactly which sounds, or what proportion of sounds, are deliberately produced to convey information to other dolphins. Bottlenose dolphins produce whistles that seem to be specific to the individual. These may be 'signature whistles' that the animals use to identify themselves or call each other. However, the whistles vary and individuals mimic each other, so it cannot be assumed that these sounds definitely constitute a greeting. It is not yet known if other species exhibit the same behaviour.

As well as listening to their natural sounds, researchers have tried to elucidate the language proficiency of dolphins by testing them according to the human model. Bottlenose dolphins can quickly and accurately grasp the implication of simple sentences. They have demonstrated an understanding of both the meaning of words (semantics), and the structure of sentences (syntax). But these findings, although fascinating, do not amount to evidence of language. Another moot point is whether there is any real value in foisting human language structures upon another species and analysing their ability to work with them. These studies do, however, indicate that dolphins have advanced skills of comprehension. It can only be assumed that a higher level of communication takes place between dolphins than between dolphins and humans. All things considered, it appears that dolphin vocalisations are not sufficiently complex to support anything approaching a human language, but it could well be that we simply do not yet know how to listen.

Another compelling aspect of intelligence is self-awareness. In experiments conducted in the USA captive bottlenose dolphins became the first non-primates to pass the mirror test of self-recognition. The dolphins' bodies were marked with zinc oxide cream or non-toxic marker pens and a mirror placed in their tank. The dolphins reacted by examining the marks; they seemed to be aware that they were seeing their own reflection, rather than another dolphin. Human babies do not recognise themselves in mirrors until they are at least 18 months old and this development usually heralds the early stages of a sense of self, introspection and the ability to perceive the mental states of others. Again the broader implications of the experiments' success with dolphins can only be speculated upon.

AS YET THERE IS NO CONSENSUS on the nature and magnitude of cetacean intelligence. To generalise is inappropriate; there are over 80 species of whale and dolphin and their cognitive capacities are bound to differ. 'Intelligence' cannot be universally defined for these animals or any others – it is a composite of many different 'intelligences' that have evolved in response to countless influences including a particular species' habitat, lifestyle and social structure.

It seems extremely unlikely that cetaceans are the super intelligent beings that John Lilly believed them to be. But there is no doubt that compared with the majority of mammals these are brainy beasts. Their underwater world is so unlike ours, and exerts such different demands, that their intelligence would almost certainly take a very different form. Debates about intelligence help us to understand other animals, and they inform opinion about our treatment of them. If cetaceans are especially intelligent, should we hunt them and should we keep them in captivity? We have a long way to go before we truly understand the cetacean mind, and how best to apply that understanding to our relationship with them.

A happy ending?

On the future for whales and dolphins

FOR MANY PEOPLE 'save the whales' is a cherished cause and almost synonymous with 'conservation of nature'. But the evidence shows that whales, along with dolphins and porpoises, are far from saved. Not all the news is bad; populations of gray, humpback and sperm whales that were almost exterminated by whalers are making a comeback, demonstrating what can be achieved if seas are kept healthy and threats minimised. But for the majority of cetaceans the future looks uncertain.

The global human population is growing inexorably. It is estimated that by 2070 a total of 9 billion people will inhabit our planet – 50% more than are alive today. As societies expand and industrialise, and technology becomes ever more sophisticated, the exploitation of marine resources will inevitably increase. The 21st century will almost certainly see unprecedented levels of human activity in the world's oceans. It is likely that relatively inaccessible regions, including the abyssal depths of the high seas, will be opened up for use.

At present the most spirited debate about the future for cetaceans is focused on moves to legalise commercial whaling. This, however, is not the greatest danger — there are other threats whose potential impact is truly calamitous. Whales and dolphins might starve en masse if their prey fail to thrive in warming seas; they may fall victim to infectious diseases if those higher temperatures combine with chemical pollutants to weaken their immune systems; their habitat could become too degraded to support life; they may be deafened and disoriented by man-made noise; and they swim in constant danger of being struck by a ship or entangled in a fishing net.

Scientists often appraise environmental problems and their consequences independently, but in nature they combine. Little is known about how these various perils interact and exacerbate one another, but it is possible to envisage a tipping point at which their collective strength becomes overwhelming. Despite their often colossal sizes, cetaceans are especially vulnerable to being wiped out by external forces. As long-living, slow-breeding animals, their existence is rendered precarious because it is biologically impossible for numbers to rebound quickly, even if the source of danger is removed. Therefore, active measures to protect cetaceans need to be taken if we want to safeguard their future. Before we can effectively tackle these mounting pressures, we need first to reconsider our sometimes peculiar and contradictory attitudes towards cetaceans and the wider marine environment.

ONE OF THE MOST POSITIVE developments in our relationship with cetaceans is the rising popularity of whale watching. As a benign form of economic exploitation, it chimes comfortably with conservation objectives to preserve whales and dolphins. Whale watching is big business. With opportunities to observe river dolphins from wooden rafts in the Amazon, kayak among orcas in Canada and helicopter over diving sperm whales in New Zealand, more people are encountering whales and dolphins in the wild than ever before. Enterprises have sprung up in at least 87 countries and overseas territories, with over nine million whale watchers generating revenue of US$1 billion a year. As entrepreneurs flock to grab a piece of the action, growth is predicted to continue for the foreseeable future.

The whale-watching industry creates jobs, provides a significant and sustainable source of income for coastal communities, and stimulates public enthusiasm for whales, dolphins and the marine environment. Some conservationists espouse the argument

Kayaking with gray whales in Baja California.

that whale watching offers a direct and viable economic alternative to whale hunting. They reason that a whale is worth considerably more alive than it is dead, while the income generated by tourism is distributed more equably through communities than the profits of whaling. Pro-whalers contend that whaling and whale watching are not mutually exclusive pursuits but can co-exist peaceably when whales are abundant, different species are targeted, or when the two activities take place in geographically separate areas. Indeed all three of the current whaling nations – Japan, Norway and Iceland – do sustain whale-watching industries.

The birthplace of whale watching is the Cabrillo National Monument in San Diego, USA, a park that commemorates the first arrival of a European expedition on America's west coast. In 1950 it was designated as a lookout from which the public could observe gray whales on their southerly winter migration. At the time scientists were just starting to document the species' remarkable recovery from whaling. In its first year the spectacle attracted 10,000 visitors. Five years later, enthusiasts were given the opportunity to enjoy a closer encounter with gray whales when a small outfit began offering boat trips for US$1. The venture was a great success and over the following decade similar enterprises proliferated along the USA's west coast. In 1971 whale watching arrived on the eastern seaboard when the Montreal Zoological Society began running trips down the St Lawrence river to view fin, minke and beluga whales.

By the late 1970s whale watching had spread to Hawaii and New England, areas that are blessed with healthy populations of humpback whales. More active at the surface than other species, humpbacks frequently approach boats, slap their tails and breach acrobatically, sometimes hurling their giant bodies clear of the water. Various explanations for this prodigious leaping have been proposed: the whales may be communicating with each other, surveying the view, trying to dislodge external parasites such as barnacles and suckerfish, or simply having fun. Whatever the reason, their athleticism delights spectators and provides unrivalled photo opportunities. Thus the humpback whale caused public participation to soar, transforming whale watching from a homespun tourism venture into a major industry.

New England is widely viewed as a model of what whale watching can achieve if it is conducted with science and conservation goals, as well as profits, in mind. From early on local operators formed collaborative partnerships with cetacean researchers. The scientists act as on-board naturalists, adding value to the trips by providing informative commentaries and answering passengers' questions. In return they use their time on the water to carry out their own research. In this way some whale-watching companies have cooperated with biologists to establish the North Atlantic Humpback Whale Catalogue, a photographic inventory of more than 6000 whales.

The industry has also contributed to the protection of the animals on which it depends. New England's humpback whales congregate on inshore feeding grounds bordered by the curving hook of Cape Cod where they are often joined by North Atlantic right whales, fin whales, minke whales and sometimes long-finned pilot whales and Atlantic white-sided dolphins. The area, once plundered by the whalers of nearby Nantucket, was declared the Stellwagen Bank National Marine Sanctuary in 1992. By that time over four million people had been to see the whales; the combined efforts of the public and whale-watching operators provided the campaign for the sanctuary with crucial impetus.

By the 1990s whale watching was booming in the Canary Islands, Australia, New Zealand, South Africa, Japan, Norway, Iceland and a number of other countries. In most locations entertainment rather than education is emphasised and there is some debate as to whether whale watching is always a force for good. Like all forms of tourism, it can have a downside. Some conservationists are concerned that the industry promotes travel on fuel-hungry planes and boats that can add significant amounts of carbon dioxide to the atmosphere and contribute towards climate change. On a more local level, whale watching is a competitive industry and, unsurprisingly, the pressures of commerce sometimes conflict with the needs of the animals. Without regulation, boat traffic can become intensive and unrelenting, disrupting whales and dolphins while they feed, rest, nurse their young and socialise. The vast majority of companies act responsibly but some unscrupulous operators may deliberately harass the animals, encouraging dolphins to bow-ride or provoking

Whale watchers occasionally fail to act responsibly; this humpback whale is completely surrounded and probably distressed.

whales to breach, tail slap or make defensive rushes past the boat. Between 1995 and 2004, a series of international workshops examined the impact of whale watching on whales. It was concluded that the industry did not cause harm but that caution was necessary – negative effects might take years to show up, and although whale watching does not reduce a whale's ability to survive, it might diminish its quality of life.

There are no international rules governing the practice of whale watching and it would be impossible to develop protocols appropriate to all species and situations. In some parts of the world tight regulations are backed up by legal enforcement. In others, compliance may be inadequately enforced or regulations may consist of purely voluntary codes of conduct. Guidelines generally counsel operators to minimise speed and noise, limit approach distances – often to a fairly arbitrary 100 m (300 ft), and to refrain from startling, pursuing, encircling or separating the animals. The International Whaling Commission (IWC) adopted a whale-watching resolution in 1993. The move was propelled by a number of members who consider it both appropriate and important that the Commission creates links with the industry since its remit is to oversee the use of cetacean resources.

Animal welfare concerns are heightened when tourists are offered the chance to swim with wild dolphins and whales – opportunities for which are increasing. It is entirely understandable that some cetacean admirers crave these exhilarating and memorable interactions, but the practice may not be safe for swimmers or in the best interests of the animals. In some cases the animals are enticed to participate with food. If provisioning is uncontrolled it could cause them to abandon and lose their natural foraging abilities, while begging behaviours could lead to aggression.

The most established site for interactions between humans and wild cetaceans is at Monkey Mia on Australia's west coast.

Diving with bottlenose dolphins in the Caribbean (top). Monkey Mia's dolphins receiving fishy treats (bottom).

Since the 1960s bottlenose dolphins have been accepting hand-outs of fish from tourists wading in the crystal blue, knee-deep water. Their friendly behaviour has spawned a multi-million dollar industry. But the association has a troubled history. During the 1980s an unusually high number of juvenile dolphins died. Their mothers were spending all day soliciting food in the shallows and were neglecting to suckle their offspring. The young calves became emaciated and weak and vulnerable to disease and shark attacks. The local wildlife authorities responded by adopting various changes. Nowadays feeding takes place only in the mornings and under strict supervision by rangers, adults are strictly rationed and obliged to find at least three-quarters of their daily requirements by foraging, and calves are not fed at all. This approach has proved extremely successful in eliminating the problems but it is possible that similar situations will arise in other locations if feeding is not carefully regulated. Little can be determined with certainty until more time passes and more research is carried out.

THE MOST FUNDAMENTAL TOOL for addressing the myriad threats to cetaceans is the law. Generally speaking, those species living in rivers, estuaries and along coastlines require national or regional legislation. Those that dwell in the high seas and migrate between oceans need international legislation. Many local projects focus on a single species, primarily those that are seriously endangered. While their salvation seems an obvious priority, the circumstances that depleted their populations in the first place need to be tackled as they will eventually affect other species. Other campaigns confront specific issues such as noise pollution or bycatch. Again while this may be the best approach in some cases, the threats in question may not be operating in isolation.

The sea presents a much greater challenge than the land when it comes to establishing protected reserves. It has depth as well as area, and is vast and dynamic. Although it does contain natural boundaries such as those between water of different temperatures, or salinities, unlike terrestrial perimeters they are constantly shifting. Furthermore, marine creatures sometimes move their feeding and breeding grounds. For these reasons marine protection may need to be designed with in-built flexibility and the capacity to adjust margins over time. The drafting of legislation that allows for continual monitoring and fine-tuning would represent a departure from existing models that were developed on land and use fixed geographical borders.

The most far-reaching and beneficial solutions are those that seek to conserve entire ecosystems. To do that it is necessary to take a broad perspective and consider the health of all the animals, plants and microorganisms in an area. Multilateral initiatives like these must address the whole range of human activities that might undermine those populations. Their success will probably depend upon changing patterns of human behaviour, so the involvement and agreement of all the people who use that ecosystem will be essential. A method increasingly used in marine conservation is the designation of special regions that are subject to certain regulations. Often referred to as 'marine protected areas,' these refuges vary greatly in size from small estuaries to large tracts of ocean.

In 2005 a major study conducted by Erich Hoyt on behalf of the Whale and Dolphin Conservation Society identified over 500 existing or proposed marine protected areas in which cetaceans are found. Additionally, at least 19 countries have declared their national waters as sanctuaries for whales and dolphins since the 1970s. Although these are very positive measures, the level of protection granted varies and the vast majority of reserves do not provide year-round cover for the roughly 80% of cetaceans that spend at least some of their lives on the high seas, outside national jurisdiction.

There are two vast whale sanctuaries on the high seas, both of which were established by the IWC. The Indian Ocean Sanctuary, inaugurated in 1979, covers the entire ocean and protects the mating and calving grounds, and some feeding grounds, of all the southern hemisphere baleen whales and sperm whales. The Southern Ocean Sanctuary came into being 15 years later. It is contiguous with the Indian Ocean Sanctuary and embraces the Antarctic feeding grounds of all the great whales except Bryde's whale, which does not stray that far south.

The IWC sanctuaries are important but they are not considered role models for conservation practice because neither offers comprehensive security. In both cases great whales are protected from commercial whaling but they, and the many small cetaceans that fall outside the auspices of the IWC, are still prone to the impacts of pollution, fisheries and shipping, while Japan conducts scientific whaling within the boundaries of the Southern Ocean Sanctuary. Such shortcomings are not uncommon; the ambitions of many conservation schemes look great on paper but are inadequate in practice. This is the case with the Biosphere Reserve, established by Mexico in the upper Gulf of California in 1993 to protect the critically endangered vaquita. Hunting of the porpoise is prohibited, but the remaining individuals continue to die as bycatch in fishing nets.

The IWC is a focus for work on the conservation of cetaceans on the high seas but its power is limited; its remit extends to only a handful of the world's 85 species, decisions taken are not necessarily binding, and the conflicting objectives of its members can curb progress. The outlook for its conservation projects is also uncertain – if Japan, Norway and their pro-whaling allies continue to gain ascendancy, they might seek to stifle this aspect of the Commission's work. Instead, hope for the future of cetacean conservation lies increasingly in action by other organisations. Fortunately a number of international conventions and institutions are starting to play a role. Perhaps the most important of these is UNCLOS, the wide-ranging United Nations Convention of the Law of the Sea, which came into force in 1994. With regard to cetaceans, the treaty instructs member states to "work through the appropriate international organisations for their conservation, management and study". This sounds convincing but leaves governments considerable leeway to decide what, in practice, the text means and how they should act on it. Other international treaties that contribute to the defence of cetaceans are the Convention on Biological Diversity – the first comprehensive international agreement committing governments to conserve plants and animals and sustain biodiversity – and the Convention on the Conservation of Migratory Species of Wild Animals, which has relevance to all the species that swim across national boundaries.

There are also promising new developments taking place in the field of regional cetacean conservation, exemplified by The Pelagos Sanctuary for Mediterranean Marine Mammals. Designated in 1999 by the governments of Italy, France and Monaco, the sanctuary spans 87,000 sq km (36,000 sq miles) and encompasses both national waters and high-sea zones. It is home to fin whales, sperm whales and various dolphins as well as a rich diversity of fish species. For conservationists this project sets an exciting precedent of nations cooperating to safeguard the whales, dolphins and other creatures of the high seas.

Making conservation decisions is far from simple at the best of times. Where whales and dolphins are concerned the challenges are amplified because there are large gaps in our knowledge of how and where they feed, breed, raise their calves and migrate. In recent years there has been growing interest in applying the 'precautionary principle' to management issues. The precautionary principle represents a philosophical shift that incorporates uncertainty into policy-making. In the past, lack of clear scientific evidence frequently impeded action. Conservation advocates were required to prove, unequivocally, that users of natural resources were causing harm before moves could be made to stop them. Although there is persuasive logic in gaining a full understanding of cause and effect before making decisions, delay can be potentially catastrophic. When the precautionary principle is applied the burden of proof is reversed. The onus falls on users to demonstrate that their activities are not detrimental before they are permitted to proceed.

Application of the precautionary principle is especially relevant to the conservation of cetaceans because they are so hard to study. The World Conservation Union (IUCN) catalogues almost 50% of cetacean species as data deficient – we simply do not know how their populations fare. This lack of information could seriously obstruct efforts to protect them, unless the precautionary principle is applied.

THE LAST 50 YEARS have seen a dramatic change in attitudes towards whales and dolphins. Once viewed as a purely economic resource, they are now greatly appreciated for their intrinsic values. Mechanisms for their conservation have made huge strides but despite this their future is far from secure. The plight of many species is in fact worsening as their ocean home faces an intensifying onslaught. The changing fortunes of cetaceans are of profound consequence. As top predators, their status acts as a barometer of the health of the entire marine ecosystem. A decline in numbers reflects the mounting pressures that they, their prey and their environment are under.

The enduring popularity of whales and dolphins does not make them more important than less appealing creatures, but it is something that can be capitalised upon. Cetaceans provide a compelling focus for education about the marine environment and the human activities that intrude on their lives. As charismatic symbols of the sea they can be used to encourage a culture of sustainability in which biodiversity is valued and conserved.

Anyone who was alive in the 1960s would have used products containing whale oil, probably without giving it a second thought. Ways of thinking, particularly about commercial whaling, have altered radically in many countries in a short space of time and it cannot be assumed that the rest of the world will keep pace. But even where attitudes have changed, they have not necessarily been matched by action. If we really want to 'save the whales' we cannot care complacently. At present our values are sometimes contradictory. We seem to have a boundless capacity to form emotional attachments to individual animals – as exemplified by the public's heartfelt reaction to the London whale, to Keiko, and to the many individuals whose live stranding unfailingly provokes an energetic and compassionate response. But even when such efforts are successful, they make only a tiny difference in a world of big problems.

The reconciliation of our sometimes illogical relationship to the natural world is one of the challenges of the future. We need to increase understanding and broaden our perspective to embrace not only distressed individuals but all the members of their species and the entire marine ecosystem that sustains them. Awareness of the hundreds of thousands of whales and dolphins that die in fishing nets every year, and the poisonous chemicals and obliterating noise we generate, should lead us to reconsider the assumption that our commercial and recreational use of the oceans is cost-free and sacrosanct.

Most cetaceans do not confine themselves to national borders so the task at hand is to find globally acceptable conservation ideals. These must be backed up by the international will to implement them. There is no single strategy or organisation that can ensure the health of the marine environment, and there are no quick fix solutions. If conservation initiatives are to succeed they must be multi-faceted and versatile enough to accommodate the needs of both people and nature. As knowledge of the lives of cetaceans and our impact upon them becomes ever more detailed, we are increasingly well placed to act. Despite the enormity of the problems faced, there is room for hope that in the end we will find a way to share our world with these eternally fascinating, mysterious and wonderful creatures – the whales, dolphins and porpoises.

Further information

Recommended reading

A History of World Whaling, D. Francis. Viking/Allen Lane, 1990.
A colourful examination of the development of the whaling industry.

At the Water's Edge: Fish with Fingers, Whales with Legs, C. Zimmer. Touchstone, 1999.
A gripping account of life in ancient seas and how the first whales evolved to live in them.

Beluga Days, N. Lord. Counterpoint Press, 2004.
One woman's quest to discover what has happened to the beluga whales of Alaska's Cook Inlet.

Encyclopedia of Marine Mammals, W. F. Perrin, B. Würsig and J.G.M Thewissen (eds). Academic Press Inc, 2002.
An indispensable resource covering everything from ambergris to zooplankton.

In the Heart of the Sea: The Epic True Story that Inspired 'Moby Dick', N. Philbrick. HarperCollins, 2001.
The compelling tale of the sinking of the *Essex* brilliantly evokes the whaling culture of 19th-century Nantucket.

Killers of Eden, T. Mead. Vantage Press, 1994.
The story of the remarkable alliance between whalers and orcas that developed in Eden, Australia.

Man and Dolphin, J. C. Lilly. Gollancz, 1962.
Lilly's first foray into inter-species communication.

Marine Protected Areas for Whales, Dolphins and Porpoises: A World Handbook for Cetacean Habitat Conservation, E. Hoyt. Earthscan Publications Ltd, 2004.
An in-depth study of the principles and practice of creating marine protected areas for cetaceans.

Men & Whales, R. Ellis. Lyons Press, 1999.
The most comprehensive work on whaling, this book investigates the industry throughout history and around the world.

So Remorseless a Havoc: Of Dolphins, Whales and Men, R. McNally. Little, Brown, 1981.
Although dated, this is a very readable look at whaling, literature and our relationship with whales and dolphins.

Sperm Whales: Social Evolution in the Ocean, H. Whitehead. University of Chicago Press, 2003.
The definitive portrait of this charismatic animal.

The Conservation of Whales and Dolphins: Science and Practice, M. P. Simmonds and J. D. Hutchinson (eds). John Wiley & Sons Inc, 1996.
A comprehensive survey of the problems faced by whales and dolphins, and how they might be solved.

The Marine Mammals of the North-western Coast of North America: Described and Illustrated, Together with an Account of the American Whale-fishery, C. M. Scammon. Peter Smith Publishers Inc, 1968.
A first-hand, illustrated report from the whaler turned artist.

Whales, Dolphins & Porpoises, M. Carwardine, E. Hoyt, R. Ewan Fordyce and P. Gill. Time Life Education, 1998.
A valuable reference source plus field notes for whale watchers.

Whales, Ice and Men: The History of Whaling in the Western Arctic, John Bockstoce. University of Washington Press, 1995.
A superbly researched chronicle of America's whaling adventures in the far north.

Recommended websites

American Cetacean Society – www.acsonline.org
The oldest cetacean conservation group in the world, the ACS campaigns on environmental issues and offers free educational resources.

Baiji.org – www.baiji.org
An organisation dedicated to saving the Chinese river dolphin.

Dolphin Institute – www.dolphin-institute.org
Research institute that focuses on dolphin behaviour and intelligence, and humpback whales.

Environmental Investigation Agency – www.eia-international.org/campaigns/species/cetaceans
Specialising in highly-regarded and sometimes undercover investigative work, the EIA runs a number of campaigns to protect whales and dolphins.

Greenpeace – www.greenpeace.org/international/campaigns/save-our-seas-2/save-the-whales
Their campaign to save the whales.

High North Alliance – www.highnorth.no
This pro-whaling alliance has accumulated a large online library in support of their cause.

Humane Society of the United States – www.hsus.org/marine_mammals
HSUS campaigns on a wide range of environmental problems that affect cetaceans and other marine mammals.

Institute of Cetacean Research – www.icrwhale.org/eng-index
Japan's main whaling research body.

International Whaling Commission – www.iwcoffice.org
With details of the ICRW , information on whale stocks and meeting reports.

IUCN Red List – www.iucnredlist.org
The key source for information on the conservation status of all the world's whales and dolphins.

New Bedford Whaling Museum – www.whalingmuseum.org
The largest American whaling museum has fantastic archives and other resources available online.

North Atlantic Right Whale Consortium – www.rightwhaleweb.org
Information on right whale research and conservation strategies.

Saint Lawrence Belugas Program – www.medvet.umontreal.ca/
pathologie_microbiologie/beluga/anglais/default_ang.asp
The University of Montreal's beluga research team.

Thewissen laboratory – www.neoucom.edu/depts/anat/thewissen/
whale_origins
Research into the evolution of whales.

US Marine Mammal Navy Program – www.spawar.navy.mil/sandiego/
technology/mammals/
The roles of marine mammals in the military and methods of animal training.

Whale and Dolphin Conservation Society – www.wdcs.org
The leading organisation dedicated to the conservation and welfare of whales
and dolphins worldwide. Their website offers extensive resources and ideas on
how to get involved.

WhaleNet – http://whale.wheelock.edu/
Offers links to lots of educational resources, plus the chance to email questions to scientists.

Recommended reports

A lot of the information on environmental and welfare issues relating to
cetaceans has been published in the form of scientific and conservation reports.
These are all available online or as hard copies from the relevant organisations.

A Brief Overview of Global Environmental Change and Its Impact on Cetaceans.
Environmental Investigation Agency, 21 pp., 1999.

Biting the Hand That Feeds: The Case Against Dolphin Petting Pools. Whale and Dolphin
Conservation Society and the Humane Society of the United States, 12 pp., 2003.

Captive Orcas: Dying to Entertain You. Whale and Dolphin Conservation Society,
101 pp., 2001.

*Dolphins, Whales and Porpoises: 2002–2010 Conservation Action Plan for the World's
Cetaceans.* The World Conservation Union's (IUCN) Cetacean Specialist
Group, 147 pp., 2003.

Global Chemical Pollution and the Hunting of Whales, Dolphins and Porpoises. Environmental Investigation Agency, 8 pp., 2004.

Hunted Dead or Still Alive – A Report on the Cruelty of Whaling. Whale and Dolphin Conservation Society and the Humane Society of the United States, 16 pp., 2003.

IWC Survival Kit. High North Alliance, 28 pp., 2006.

Japan's Whale Research Program Under Special Permit in the Antarctic (JARPA). Institute of Cetacean Research, 57 pp., 2006.

Mercury Rising: The Sale of Polluted Whale, Dolphin and Porpoise Meat in Japan. Environmental Investigation Agency, 14 pp., 2003.

Oceans of Noise. Whale and Dolphin Conservation Society, 168 pp., 2004.

Review of the Scientific Justifications for Maintaining Cetaceans in Captivity. Whale and Dolphin Conservation Society, 45 pp., 1998.

Revised Management Strategy: A Question of Confidence. Whale and Dolphin Conservation Society, ProWildlife and the Humane Society International, 20 pp., 2005.

Sounding the Depths II: The Rising Toll of Sonar, Shipping and Industrial Ocean Noise on Marine Life. National Resources Defence Council of the United States, 84 pp., 2005.

The Case Against Marine Mammals in Captivity. Humane Society of the United States and the World Society for the Protection of Animals, 75 pp., 2006.

The Conservation of Whales in the 21ˢᵗ Century. The Government of New Zealand's Department of Conservation, 34 pp., 2004.

The Net Effect? A Review of Cetacean Bycatch in Pelagic Trawls and Other Fisheries in the North-east Atlantic. A Whale and Dolphin Conservation Society report for Greenpeace, 74 pp., 2004.

The Second Phase of Japan's Whale Research Program in the Western North Pacific (JARPN II). Institute of Cetacean Research, 51 pp., 2006.

Whales Competing? An Analysis of the Claim that Some Whales Eat so Much that They Threaten Fisheries and the Survival of Other Whales. International League for the Protection of Cetaceans, 86 pp., 2006.

Why Whale Research? The Institute of Cetacean Research, 12 pp., 2005.

Index

Bold page numbers indicate main references to cetacean species.

Picture Credits